Leadership Secrets of the 10% Club:

Right in the Heart...

Marcus P. Mitchell

4|5|14
Roe

Copyright © 2014 Marcus P. Mitchell

1st Edition

Published by
'If, And or But' Publishing Company
Battle Creek, Michigan USA
www.ifandorbutpublishing.com

ISBN-13: 978-1495990595
ISBN-10: 1495990591

Cover photos are licensed images through BigStockPhotos.com. License obtained by *If, And or But Publishing* in 2014.

Table of Contents

To my parents.
A special 'Thank you' to both of you.
You instilled in me a great sense of confidence
and self sufficiency. You will always be awesome
and you are my heroes. I learned my most valuable
life lessons from you. You are next to God.
I love you both.

✥Introduction✥

When one begins to write a book about leadership, it is prudent to ask as a first question: *What is leadership?* There are many texts and viewpoints on this topic if you venture into exploring your local bookstores and the online blogosphere. A great deal of information is available for study out there on the subject, but one can still be left with the same unanswered question: *What is leadership?* What makes a person *a good leader?*

Perhaps the subject is best explored from a contrary viewpoint. Instead of asking the direct question on what leadership is. One could better approach discovery of the answer by turning this question around. What if one were to seek to understand first *what leadership is not?* Therein lays an approach that many could rally behind with answers as we have all experienced or witnessed bad leadership at some point in our lives. We knew this intuitively, even if we had no precise definition for leadership.

Let's explore this question instead: *What is leadership not?*

Leadership is *not* sitting in an office issuing orders to the masses behind a closed door. It is not who can overpower another, or shout the loudest either. It does not consist of belittling others, being the most critical or engaging in antisocial behavior. Nor is leadership for the elite or egotistical, far removed from the struggles of day to day living. No, leadership does not draw its power from the ugly side of man's experience or behavior. Leadership is none of those things.

Leadership is not avoidance or neglect of problems. It is not harming others for personal gain. It is not being a bully, or threatening others. And leadership is most certainly not using ones position to feather ones nest at the expense of the group one is serving. These things are plain to see. People in positions of power that do these types of things live miserable existences. They spend their lives in constant fear or suspicion of others, which is quite the opposite of leadership qualities.

True leadership is founded on the roots of compassion and understanding for the people one is leading. It is driven by a purpose to arrive at the summit on the horizon. It is love for ones fellows, and the skills to tap into the energy of the true believers who follow you.

Perhaps the best example I can give comes from a series of events which happened to me and thus began my discoveries into the founding core principles presented in this book.

In the early 1980's I was a young scientist working for a major pharmaceutical company. One day our CEO called a meeting of all staff, and explained in detail that the entire pharmaceutical industry was going through a series of mergers. At that time there were approximately 300 such companies in the U.S. alone and he was predicting that within 10 years there would be but a handful remaining as a result of all the corporate mergers. He stated that our pending merger was the first of many, but in the end we would be one of the few independent companies left.

During the time the CEO was making these points known; an older colleague turned to me and muttered conspiratorially *"That's a load of crap!"* Almost immediately following his statement, the CEO addressed the group and said *"Now, I know there are 10% of you that will never believe anything I say..."* and the entire room erupted into laughter over the irony and timing of the rejoinder.

Later on in the week that same colleague began what he coined affectionately *'The 10% Club'*. He would call everyone on the team and tell them 'there was a 10% Club meeting today'. Essentially this meant that we would all meet at a local bar after work. It was an inside joke among my co-workers, but ultimately a decade later that visionary CEO was proven right. The entire industry changed, and his ability to calculate and prepare for the future made our company one of a handful independently left standing 10 years later.

The lesson I learned from this experience was that there was a human dynamic to managing people. If one were to place it into context of a Bell Curve, it would be seen that 10% will never believe and will drag behind. 80% will be spectators, and will be ready to follow, but reluctant to lead. The final 10% will be the true believers and pioneers and shift the entire Bell Curve along the lines of progress.

Learning how to shift ones thinking and become a member of that final 10% group with the vision of a pioneer and true believer in a dream, and lead others forward towards that ideal is what this book is about.

Not everyone will become a leader, although the power resides within them. Some will lag behind and proclaim that it cannot be done and proclaim that *'all is impossible'* and instead go to the bar and complain with others of like mind. Many more will simply wait for another to carry the torch so that they can follow. True leadership consists of that remaining 10% who are at their core *true believers* that can envision the future, and *accomplish the impossible.*

Renowned author and scholar William Bennis once wrote: *"Leadership is the capacity to translate vision into reality".* This book will serve as a guide to a greater understanding of leadership, and empower the reader with the inspiration to translate their own vision into reality and achieve the impossible for any group they choose to lead.

I have accumulated a wide and, some would say, eclectic and diverse range of experiences fueled by one overarching thought: *To Find the Truth.* This quest has led me down many paths. As you will read, I have worked in corporate America and have often referred to myself as a *"Corporate Baby"* where I witnessed corporate greed, corporate detachment, corporate philanthropy, and corporate humanitarianism.

I have also worked for and with a variety of not-for-profit organizations where I saw firsthand the benefits that these organizations offer to the public at large, but I also witnessed firsthand the greed, exploitation and elitism they can be subjected to.

I have also worked with government learning to navigate the national bureaucracy and also learned the hurdles and obstacles that an ill-informed citizen would face, at the same time befriending dedicated public servants who helped thousands overcome those barriers.

Throughout my life I have been truly blessed to have been offered these experiences and I feel a profound obligation, a calling, to share what I have learned.

This book has been written and designed to help people by providing insights and some basic philosophies which have helped me to navigate our capitalist society, through interaction with corporations, organizations, not-for-profit entities, federal, state and municipal governments, agencies, citizens groups, churches, non-governmental organizations, grassroots efforts, chambers of commerce, and even student groups. I have learned and experienced a lot from each one.

I urge readers to follow each section of this book. The sections are divided into groupings of subcategories following a logical progression to give a comprehensive overview of strategies that allow for easy study and more importantly, implementation. One thing that I have learned about a profound truth is this: *Implementation of a plan is King.* Proper planning is very important, and implementation is paramount.

One of the many mottos I have used in countless groups I have led is simply *"Make It Happen!"* Such is the foundation of this book. Leadership is about inspiring others to greatness, as well as accomplishing great things.

I have interwoven throughout the pages of this book my personal life stories and experiences to illustrate points at various times. These events did happen, and were instrumental in my personal development as a leader. I share this wisdom with you within these pages. I hope to engage you in discovering the various aspects of leadership, and what it takes to be a great leader.

I have included wisdom from great, inspiring people whose messages I have quoted and included within these pages; together may we awaken the leader in you, right in the heart...

Chapter One:
Courage & Leadership

"Men make history and not the other way around. In periods where there is no leadership, society stands still. Progress occurs when courageous, skillful leaders seize the opportunity to change things for the better."

~ Harry S. Truman

To climb to that elite 10% group of people who can lead effectively requires courage of a special nature. Courage could best be defined as: *having the mental and moral strength to venture forward, persevere and withstand danger, fear or difficulty.* It has also been defined as: *that ability to do something that frightens one.*

However perhaps the easier way to look at courage is to go to its root word in Latin which is *cor* which translates into *heart.* Having courage was thought to come from the heart, the seat of all feelings, and it meant one had strength to face the challenges of adversity. Such is the climate of leadership.

An essential part of courage and leadership is being willing to do what 95% of people might not do. Taking the position that one can accomplish the impossible or improbable as the leader of a group requires heart. To defy the group agreement of the 95% who say it cannot be done and going forward to make the task a reality is both bold and sometimes astonishing to the non-believers. However, that is the true essence of leadership.

Think it through

"A true leader has the confidence to stand alone, the courage to make tough decisions, and the compassion to listen to the needs of others. He does not set out to be a leader, but becomes one by the equality of his actions and the integrity of his intent."
~Douglas MacArthur

A courageous leader takes a moment to think through a decision before committing, so as to make the best possible decision for the survival and expansion of the group. Spend some time thinking on the steps that lie ahead, and prepare for the possibilities of unexpected obstacles.

A major part of the challenge of a leader is having the courage to make tough decisions, and as Douglas MacArthur stated in the above quote, is having the *compassion to listen* and factor in the needs of others.

The people impacted by a leader's decision are not just those in his own organization, but as in non-profit organizations and companies, it is the public one is serving.

The Dangers of Second Guessing Oneself

"A man who wants to lead the orchestra must turn his back on the crowd."

~ Max Lucado

I have found that some leaders will not move unless they take a *survey* or *poll*, and thus, are not creating the movement or music. They will frequently wait to find out what others think on the matter before taking action. In doing so, they are not using their own interpretive powers of a situation, but instead are being led by the masses.

Unless a leader can turn his or her back to the allure of peer pressure and stand alone to lead the orchestra (the 10%), he or she will be unable to achieve the great music for all to enjoy and benefit from. Likewise, they will never experience that crescendo of success, nor any standing ovation for their achievements.

A position of leadership can have many ups and downs. A dangerous train of thinking that a leader can stumble into like a snare trap is to begin to question their own decisions with '*Am I wrong?*'

The danger in this type of thinking is that the leader begins to look inward and backward at the past, instead of looking outward and forward towards the future.

Forward thinking and focusing on the future is the way to accomplishment and completion of goals. Backward thinking and pondering one's inadequacies is a quagmire that one will sink into and bring to a halt any progress or advancement.

If you want to experience your universe shrinking to the size of a tiny phone booth, question your every decision.

If you want to achieve success, have courage and be willing to accept your mistakes as they happen, but always remain focused on the future. The past cannot easily be rectified or corrected, but the future is virgin territory yet unexplored.

Keep your head up and your eyes looking boldly forward and you will find yourself on the right path.

Be Determined

"Lead me, follow me, or get out of my way."

~ General George Patton

Determination could best be defined as *'qualities that drive or make one continue trying to achieve something that is difficult'*. Being resolute and firmly focused on one's purpose is the basic fabric of determination.

As a leader one must not only have the courage to face opposition or adversity, but one must remain determined if one is ever to reach a goal.

Therefore, courage could be said to be the substance that helps one keep moving forward against all odds, and determination could be likened to the fuel that drives one. No leader ever accomplished a goal worth achieving without determination.

Courage: *Right in the Heart*

"As a leader, if you follow your heart, you will have the courage to take on any risk because your heart will lead you to the solution and avoid the risk."
~Angeline Kobe Chan

I have always been one to refrain from complaining about a situation until after I have honestly investigated and tried to offer a solution that will make matters better. I have never been one to sit back and complain from an armchair in my living room. I have to get out in the field, look for myself and do my part.

During my tenure as a director of community and economic development with the United States Senate, I took the opportunity to examine a social problem that I wanted to make an impact on: *Homelessness.*

Once I took an interest, I started to use the resources of the office to examine and research. There were a multitude of agencies and nonprofits that addressed the issue in local communities. Many of them received federal funding in the form of grants.

These grants and funding created some agencies that evolved into having multi-million dollar budgets. In my interest, I began to try to examine and discover for myself how effective these agencies were at addressing the issue of homelessness.

During my initial investigation, I noticed one small agency had a very small budget, but were managing to service more people than anyone else. My curiosity was piqued. I had to see if this agency was for real, and if so, what they were doing that was successful. If they really were not successful, I wanted to know that, too. As with any government-funded group effort, it can happen more often than not that unscrupulous individuals will try to take advantage of the situation and exploit other people. Thus, I was keen to investigate.

So I decided I was going to spend the weekend at this particular homeless shelter. I notified my office of my intentions and changed my suit into some street clothes that I used for gardening in. I bid my farewells to my colleagues in the office and made my way on foot to the shelter.

Once at the shelter, I checked in at the intake office. I found to it be a very humane operation. I had expected humiliating behavior, but that is not what I experienced. The staff treated me with nothing less than dignity and compassion.

I was allowed to take a shower and had dinner. There were hundreds of homeless men in the shelter as it was August in the middle of a heat wave. I was brought to a room where there were rows of bunk beds in an open space, and heat was sweltering. I could hear a fan blowing, but it did not feel as if the air was circulating at all.

That first night, I was lying on my bunk, making my notes mentally on the operation. A man about my age lying in the bunk next to me began to talk to me. For the purpose of this story, let's call him John.

John began to tell me his story, sharing the details of his situation with me. To this day I am not exactly sure why he decided to talk with me, as opposed to someone else. I suppose to him I looked like someone who would listen.

John had been a skilled carpenter, and he once had his own thriving business. He told me he had developed a substance abuse issue, a combination of both drinking and drugs. As he told me his story, tears were in his eyes, and to this day I will never forget the expression on his face.

He said he never dreamed he would be in this place at this point in his life, or that things would get to be this bad for him. He told me that the only thing he wanted to do was to get his wife back, whom he had lost in his downward spiral of addiction. He said he wanted to get his job back, reconcile with his wife, and rebuild their life together.

Unaware that he was talking to a department head connected with the U.S Senate, he poured his heart out about the tragedy of his life. I thought to myself lying there in that August night, that I really wanted do something to help this man.

The next morning we had a chance to use the bathroom and wash ourselves at the sink. There was a line of people formed waiting to use them. As the line moved, and I got closer to the front of the line I saw that there was one man using 3 sinks, while scores of people waited.

I stepped forward to use one of the sinks and he turned on me. He wanted to fight, and my initial impulse was that I would fight with him and my intention mounted with the desire to beat him senseless. I was appalled at his selfishness.

As I stood my ground nose to nose with this man berating him for keeping others waiting in line, another very tall man stepped out of the line and walked toward me. At first I thought I might have to fight two people, but the tall man looked at me, placed his hand gently on my shoulder and said four words to me that I will always remember: *Humble is the way.*

That's all he said, but it was enough to remind me of the real reason I was there: *to help people.* I lost my head for a moment because the man using three sinks was so inconsiderate of everyone else that I was determined to call him out on his rude behavior.

However, the tall man's words were spoken to my soul. I nodded to him and quietly got back in line. Later when we went to eat, no one sat with me. I began to wonder if people could tell that I was not homeless.

I later asked someone why no one sat with me. This man told me it was because they didn't know me. So I realized that they were no different than any other group of people. They congregate with the people they know.

I finished my day, and left the shelter completing my observations of this organization. The following night after I returned home, I began to think about my experience and how I was going to help the organization, as well as the man, John, who had told me his story.

The organization I discovered could do this incredible amount of work to help more people than anyone else with less money simply because they used sincere and honest volunteers to help do the work. There were only five people on staff who were paid, and the rest of the workers were volunteers. I found this both incredible and inspiring.

Upon returning to my office on Monday morning, I began to make preparations to help this organization. Ironically on my calendar was an appointment to meet with a man who wanted to start a training program for homeless men and women to help them learn building trades and rehabilitate houses. I told him my experiences from the weekend, and my encounter with John.

I asked him if he would come with me to the shelter so that he could give John a job. After hearing my story, he was just as excited as me to do this for him.

Together we went to the shelter and when we arrived, I asked to speak with the executive director. At the door of his office he peered at me over the rim of his glasses. I told him I was working out of an office with the United States Senate, and also that I had spent the weekend undercover at the shelter.

I let him know how impressed I was with the work he and his colleagues were doing to help so many people and that I was going to help them with the aid of the federal government. I also told him I was looking for John, relaying the story, and let him know that the man with me was going to give him a job.

The Executive Director left the office to have some of his staff go search for John. We waited for 30 minutes until he returned and said that he could not find John in the system. He explained to me that the nature of their work is that people come and go. John apparently had left the facility, and when or if he would return was unknown. That day I was not able to find John, but over the years I have continued looking.

The staff of the organization was so incredulous that I had spent the weekend at their facility, that they asked me to speak at their annual meeting and relate my experiences. The board members said they were embarrassed that somebody from outside their organization would take upon himself to stay in their facility to get an intimate view and understand what their clients had to experience. After my undercover experiment, the board instituted a policy that board members now had to spend time in the shelter themselves to experience this as I did.

I believe that's a good policy for any organization. The first-hand experience of putting yourself in the same situation of people that you're trying to help gives some small measure of what they have to endure. It's hard to imagine what it must be like for someone to live without a home for years, trying to find a meal or trying to find a job. It is hard to imagine trying to put one's life back together again when one has lost everything.

My investigation inspired the board to take a closer look and make a bigger effort to understand the value of the work that they were doing. My hat goes off to those men and women who work at shelters for a living; they are truly a special group of people.

When one is in the role of leadership, sometimes it is necessary to have courage and go forward to look and experience the organization from the inside. Not everyone is willing to take such a risk. However, if one is going to lead it is important to know how the organization is running, and sometimes it does require that one find out what is really going on. Going undercover is a great way for a leader to see an organization from the inside out.

Chapter Two:
Responsibility & Leadership

"The first responsibility of a leader is to define reality. The last is to say thank you. In between, the leader is a servant."

~Max DePree

As any business owner or manager can attest, there are times when one asks an employee or individual on their staff to do something only to find out hours later the request was ignored. Sometimes this is due to the area being busy and the employee was not able to get to the request due to heavy traffic, which sometimes can occur. However, in other times it is due to procrastination that the task was neglected.

Procrastination

"You may delay, but time will not"

~ Benjamin Franklin

An unfortunate part of mankind's nature is to procrastinate, and put off until later or even tomorrow an important task one has to hand. This extends to the people one leads. It is the responsibility of a leader to be alert for this when it happens, and persist with positive enforcement until the task is completed. Sometimes this requires making the matter an educational experience for those involved, so as to prevent such an instance from occurring again in the future.

When one truly examines the cause of procrastination, he may be alerted to the problem that can be identified and corrected. There can be many causes of this: uncertainty of the task at hand, no purpose to do it, no training or expertise for the assignment, fear of failure, distractions or home-life problems, difficulty balancing or prioritizing work load, conflicting instructions (trying to answer to 2 masters), passive-aggressive behavior, etc.

Sometimes a person can become tone deaf to receiving orders, and become mentally overloaded and then shut out all incoming instructions: *any incoming communications do not register.* Resolving this is very simple, once one recognizes this to be the case. One just needs to devote a little more time getting the person to focus with a perhaps a personal direct communication. Hand them something to touch related to the task, a file, a machine or whatever. One can even have them repeat the instructions back to you, without being overbearing or demanding about it. In essence, instead of reacting with frustration about this, identify what is before you, understand and resolve it with communication and kindness. This is brilliant leadership at its finest.

On the flip side, procrastination can be great benefit for any leader who wants to put his thoughts, concepts and plans into motion. In a group dynamic, a committee or group of people often wait for someone else to do the work.

A leader should step forward and spend the extra time and effort to do the work and establish a vision for the group. He or she can put in extra hours to prepare the agenda for a meeting or spend a weekend preparing a concept paper. Sometimes it may mean taking one hour after work to scout out a site for a fundraiser or event.

It could also mean making important phone calls to recruit potential speakers for the event, or doing the research required for the organization to make an educated decision so as to present it to the group. In this way a unique vision will be realized in a much easier manner, with a minimum debate and resistance. People at the receipt end of such delivery are most often happy to know someone else has taken the initiative, and set a course for them to follow.

In my younger days I recall being charged with a fundraising effort for a group I was involved in. The budget that was set was ridiculously low to provide food for 200 people; however it was the task I was given and the resources I had to work with.

My goal was to make this fundraising effort a huge success which meant providing a good experience for everyone who attended and which in turn, resulted in support for the organization through ticket sales for the event.

Good food is essential for a fundraising event to draw people; therefore it was to be an important part of that equation. The budget I was given worked out to approximately 50 cents per person. Thus the puzzle I had to solve in order to make the food become a draw, and the event a success was to come up with a solution that worked with this low budget.

I took inventory of my own skills and resources and determined that I am a good cook.

I decided I could prepare a meal for 200 people at 50 cents per person only if I did the cooking and prepared the food myself. This, therefore, became my mission.

The rest of the members the committee upon hearing about my solution thought the task was impossible, and all but told me outright it could not be done. I love to hear people say that a task is impossible, as it motivates me to make a point to prove that it can be done. Their statements of impossibility became my driving force do the work, and cook up a storm!

All told it took me about eight hours to prepare a very nice meal for 200 people. The outcome of the event was an overwhelming success meeting fundraising goals, and we astonished those members of the committee who thought the task impossible. As a byproduct, due to my extra effort, it catapulted me into an even higher leadership position within the organization.

In alignment with the understanding of "The 10% Club" as discussed in the introduction of this book, I have discovered that I always find myself spending three times as much of my energy on motivating the 10% of the true believers, as I know they will succeed and pull along the other remaining 80% who are followers. I have learned to dismiss of course the other 10% who will believe and follow no one when a task of utter importance needs to be done.

Sometimes, however, as in the example above, one must take hold of a task solo in order to change the minds of those who deem it to be impossible. In that way you can gain the attention of the other 80% who follow, and get them behind you.

Put Yourself in Their Shoes

"Outstanding leaders go out of their way to boost the self-esteem of their personnel. If people believe in themselves, it's amazing what they can accomplish."

~ Sam Walton

An essential ingredient of good leadership is developing the skill to put yourself in the shoes of the recipient of your orders or directions. Set aside your own bias and opinions for a moment. Place on a shelf your own concept of how things should be done, and the guidelines you follow in life. Simply take a moment and step out of your shoes, and assume the viewpoint of the other person.

How does your message sound? What was the emotion received in its delivery? Was the message clear and able to be easily understood? What was the overall flow of the experience that you delivered to that person with that communication?

Acquiring the skill to step into the other person's shoes for just a moment can help you experience and examine their perspective, as well as offer unique insight into what it means to be responsible for your own communication.

Additionally, consider for a moment that this person has their own situations in life. As a leader, one needs to take responsibility to find out what this is sometimes in order to better human relations.

Are they dealing with any external stress in life from home, family or elsewhere that is preventing them from being focused on the task at hand? How will you know if you do not inquire?

The responsibility of caring about your followers falls squarely on your shoulders as a leader. You owe it to yourself to find out how they are doing in life. Perhaps you can help them with guidance or insight to better their condition. This is all part of the responsibility of leadership.

The Caine Mutiny

"You didn't approve of his conduct as an officer. He wasn't worthy of your loyalty. So you turned on him. You ragged him. You made up songs about him. If you'd given Queeg the loyalty he needed, do you suppose the whole issue would have come up in the typhoon?"

~ Herman Wouk
(Character Lt. Barney Greenwald in the Caine Mutiny)

Whenever I consider or experience or witness a breakdown in leadership in the form of a rebellion against the leader I consider the story of the *Caine Mutiny*. The *Caine Mutiny* was a Pulitzer Prize Award winning novel by author Herman Wouk about a fictitious mutiny aboard a United States Navy military vessel, the *U.S.S. Caine* set in World War II.

The story was later adapted into a film starring Humphrey Bogart, Jose' Ferrier, Van Johnson and Fred MacMurray which won several Oscars in 1954.

As the story goes, the U.S.S. Caine was a destroyer minesweeper converted in the haste of the war from an obsolete World War I era destroyer, fitted with a ragtag crew, and set to sea. They were undisciplined, but experienced sailors. However, they did not routinely follow the routines of military life.

Their uniforms were dirty and unkempt and they did not stand to attention when an officer passed by. They performed poorly in routine Navy preparedness drills, and the ship itself was in a decaying condition. The original Captain was moved to another assignment, replaced by a new captain; Lieutenant Commander Phillip Francis Queeg who was a strict *'By the Regulations'* officer.

When Queeg assumed command he attempted to force the crew to abide by the rules and improve their performance. His officers resented him and began writing derogatory songs about him. Further complicating matters, Queeg, after assuming command lost the respect of his officers through a series of incidents, including grounding the ship upon first sailing, and attempting to cover it up, as well as nearly colliding with another Battleship on a foggy morning.

The captain had seen lots of battle in war. He was secretly suffering from what we now call post-traumatic stress disorder. In the World War II era this condition was called *battle fatigue*.

Whenever a stressful situation presented itself, the captain's ability to command collapsed as his PTSD became evident in his panic or paralyzed inaction. The crew began to undermine the captain and made efforts to report the captain's weakness to his superiors.

As the story progresses we find the ship in the midst of a typhoon and in imminent danger of capsizing in the storm. The executive officer assumes control of the ship when the captain has a breakdown under the pressure. The executive officer saves the ship and ultimately gets the ship and crew to port safely. The outcome, however, is that Queeg accuses the officers and crew of mutiny and a court-martial trial begins.

Initially, no attorney would defend the crew or officers of the Caine. Eventually one attorney, Lieutenant Barney Greenwald reluctantly takes on their case. His defense was a structured line of questioning to create a simulated pressure on the captain during the trial which causes the Captain's condition to surface for everyone to see.

Following the trial and the vindication of the officers and crew, there is a party held in celebration of the outcome. Greenwald, the defense attorney attends the party and when confronted with the jubilant crew, he tells them he feels ashamed for having destroyed Queeg on the stand. He explains that the captain was a hero and it hurt his heart to have to destroy him on the stand after he had served his country so well and then was so damaged psychologically in the process.

He further explains that Queeg was not a weak leader, despite the psychological damage he suffered from as a result of the long hard battles he had fought in the war. Instead, the attorney poses to the executive office a question: *"Steve, you're an honest man. The captain came to you and the other officers and asked for your help, didn't he?"*

Upon consideration and reflection, the executive officer says *"Yes he did ask for help and we didn't help him because we thought he was weak and he was hard on us."*

The attorney then offers a follow up question: *"Do you think if you and the other officers had helped the captain early on it would have become necessary for you to assume control of the ship in the middle of the typhoon?"*

The executive officer sadly says *"No, it would not have been necessary for me to take over the ship."* A young ensign overhearing the discussion then interjects *"So we were guilty of mutiny!"*

In reply the attorney looks upon him and says *"Now you are learning!"*

When I do crisis management efforts for companies I always try to apply this lesson. When there's a breakdown in leadership often it is a *two way street.*

Many times I have discovered ambition of aspiring leaders to be undermining the authority of the appointed leader. When we learn from this lesson of the Caine Mutiny, we must examine our own motivations and ask ourselves if we are truly focusing on success of our mission, job and the common effort. Are we truly a part of the team?

In the process of crisis management, I always give my complete support to the leader who was responsible for the effort of keeping the organization moving towards its goals.

If after examination it bears out that there are still problems with the leadership in charge, only then are other measures justified.

More often than not I find that the leader was not given full cooperation or support early on and there is an underlying resistance in the ranks.

When hearing the example of this story, people often start to nod their heads in introspection and they may question their own motivations when involved in any group effort where there are complaints about leadership.

Responsibility in leadership has many levels. It applies not just to the top leader in an organization or activity. It applies to all echelons below as well.

If one is in conflict with a leader, it is always important to step back and assume for a moment the other person's viewpoint and examine one's own role in the conflict before moving forward with a decisive action to resolve the situation.

Such is the lesson of responsibility and leadership.

Chapter Three:
The 10% Club

"Leadership is the art of getting someone else to do something you want done because he wants to do it."

~ General Dwight Eisenhower

As initially defined in the introduction, the story behind the origin of the 10% Club comes from a meeting I attended while working for a large pharmaceutical company in the early 1980's. At the risk of being redundant, I will repeat the events again in this chapter, and then elaborate more on this.

One day our CEO called a meeting of all staff, and explained in detail that the entire pharmaceutical industry was going through a series of mergers. At that time there were approximately 300 such companies in the U.S. alone and he was predicting that within 10 years there would be but a handful remaining as a result of all the corporate mergers. He stated that our pending merger was the first of many, but in the end we would be one of the few independent companies left.

During the time the CEO was making these points known; an older colleague turned to me and muttered conspiratorially *"That's a load of crap!"* Almost immediately following his statement, the CEO addressed the group and said *"Now, I know there are 10% of you that will never believe anything I say..."* and the entire room erupted into laughter over the irony and timing of the rejoinder.

Later on in the week that same colleague began what he coined affectionately *'The 10% Club'*. He would call everyone on the team and tell them 'there was a 10% Club meeting today'. Essentially this meant that we would all meet at a local bar after work.

It was an inside joke among my co-workers, but ultimately a decade later that visionary CEO was proven right. The entire industry changed, and his ability to calculate and prepare for the future made our company one of a handful independently left standing 10 years later.

The 10% Club became an expression among my colleagues of being the group that never believed. However, time has taught me from this experience that the true 10% Club is the other 10% that can embrace a vision and lead the other 80% to it.

Control & Happiness

"When I give a minister an order, I leave it to him to find the means to carry it out."

~Napoleon Bonaparte

Several years ago, there was a government study performed in search of an age-old question: *'What makes people happy?'* As is typical in government studies, lots and lots of money was spent to answer this seemingly unimportant question.

You are probably familiar with how easy it is for government to spend money on studies such as *'the sex life of a tsetse fly'*, *'is water good for you to drink'*, etc., etc., etc. Therefore a study about happiness and its origins can easily be dismissed.

This particular study was not much different from the typical cash wasting grants, except for one thing. They inadvertently found an answer from the people to this long sought after question. As expected, they spent tons of money surveying people in the quest for this answer.

Their approach was to ask an array of people from various demographics; young people, old people; Whites, African-Americans, Asians, Native Americans, Latinos and Hispanics; men, women, boys and girls; educated, uneducated; married, single, separated; wealthy, middle-class and lower income people. They conducted their survey on every group at every echelon of society they could find. Amazingly, from all of this effort, they found a most interesting and surprising answer to the core question: *'What makes people happy?'*

What do you think they found? *Was it money?* No! *Was it sex?* No! *Was it power?* No! *Was it a lifelong companion?* No! *Was it a good job?* No! *Was it lots of material things?* Most certainly not!

This governmental study found that no item on this list of assumed or expected things is what makes people happy. They found in all of their surveys that the *one thing* that makes everyone happy is *Control.*

When people feel that they are in control, *they are happy.* If you feel you're in control of your relationship, *you're happy.* When you feel that you're in control at your job, *you're happy.* When you think that you have control of your finances, *you are happy.* When you think that you are in control of your safety, and security, *you are happy.* This sense of control makes all people happy.

This is a powerful concept for any leader to understand fully. It answers a lot of questions to dynamics that many trainers and consultants tout when teaching classes on personal interaction, and group dynamics: *How do you lead people who are in fear? How do you lead people who have doubts or who have been traumatized? How do you lead people into a situation which is uncertain? How do you lead people through a process of change?*

Change is the one constant, the one thing you can always count on to occur. *Change is inevitable.* It is a constant of the universe. The leader must understand that if he provides a sense of control to the people he is leading; he has overcome 70 to 80% of an obstacle to leadership in almost any situation. (This is from my own firsthand experience)

Understanding the control paradigm can help a leader navigate difficult conversations with individuals or groups. It is also an important discovery regarding the importance of empowering those that one leads.

However, the paradigm has a catch. For all good leaders must understand: Control is *an illusion*. We don't know what will happen from one moment to the next. There are forces of nature, storms, hurricanes, earthquakes, fires, volcano eruptions. These 'Acts of God' as defined by the insurance industry are unpredictable and unforeseen circumstances that can affect everyone and anyone profoundly.

Many religions teach that only God has control. The wise leader understands that we as human beings try to obtain a sense of control, but true control is beyond our reach.

We can mitigate risk; we can plan to make a critical path easier and more efficient; we can institute measures to help us reach our goals. But these are only plans, and the wise leader must always be prepared for plans to go awry and so continue his or her leadership after the flaws of the master plan have been uncovered by unforeseen events.

A leader must constantly be aware and prepared for change as a constant condition, and be able to adjust, revise or completely overhaul extant planning when the moment presents itself. So we learn that leadership in the *10% Club* consists of not only embracing and following a vision, but also to be prepared for those moments of lost control and change that are an inevitable factor of existence.

The Dynamic of the 10% Club

"Leadership is a dynamic process that expresses our skill, our aspirations, and our essence as human beings."

~Catherine Robinson-Walker

The 10% club is a dynamic that I see at work almost everywhere: in families, in business, with community-based organizations and even among strangers on a train. The pioneers, the leaders, the 10% of true believers will pave the way and blaze a trail of success for others to witness and emulate.

Those 10% will do hard work, take risks and face potential failure. The 80% of people whom I call '*the watchers*' are the ones that desire success, but may not have the motivation, much less the resources to be in the 10%. They will however, participate in the success once they see it can be done.

In any situation, be it an emergency, a board meeting, or family conflict, a leader can utilize this concept to move any plan or project forward. The dynamics of the 10% club can cross over many levels of society, but the 80% who are *watchers* are always ready to follow the right type of leadership.

The 10% at the other end of the bell curve will move along as well, but not as quickly, and not as willingly. This group is moved simply because the majority of a group begins to move along a line of progress. They are a specialized type of potential followers who have a greater lag and typically take the rear guard.

Chapter Four:
Effective Planning

"Let your plans be dark and impenetrable as night, and when you move, fall like a thunderbolt."

~Sun Tzu, The Art of War

Plans are the road maps that guide a group towards a goal. Good planning in any group activity is vital if the group is ever to achieve a goal. A good leader is able to develop effective planning that can drive the followers along the pre-determined path in pursuit of the group goals.

A great leader should be circumspect and well-rounded. These qualities will help them overcome any unforeseen or unexpected need for changes in planning and help to ensure success if he can call on a variety of experiences and knowledge to solve problems as it relates to the plans.

Critical thinking is therefore a tremendous asset to a good leader. The broader the leader's knowledge and experience, the more he or she can gain the ability to tap into this knowledge, and use it in addressing and identifying solutions to a problem presented.

In leadership positions, I strive to be a *renaissance man.* A *'renaissance man'* or *'renaissance person'* refers to someone who develops a wide range of proficiency in skills of many fields. The European cultural rebirth during the 14th and 17th century, termed the renaissance or "Rebirth"

This term does not mean that one must become an expert or specialist in every field, but simply to have and develop a wide range of knowledge which is particularly useful in the toolbox of one in a leadership position.

In developing this proficiency and knowledge in a wide variety of areas, a good leader can be in a position to ask "why?" when something contrary to his or her knowledge is encountered. An investigation into this question will provide background and solutions, particularly if one can truly observe.

This *'renaissance man'* operating basis enables one to ask poignant questions. *Why are things being done in this manner? Why has this been defined as our goal, and not something else? Why are we choosing this path instead of another? What other similar fields of knowledge can I draw from in order to offer new insight on other possible goals?*

Research and knowledge therefore becomes an important part of reaching the solutions to a problem. Filling in the gaps in ones understanding and getting questions answered with critical data and facts is a sound practice when seeking sustainable solutions to a problem for any group.

One should not rely on motions made in a meeting to change something about an organization or group that are not supported by facts. A good leader makes a decision based on factual information. When in a leadership role, one must make decisions when one is charged with the responsibility for the well-being of a group. Solutions you propose or support must be based in facts. Organizations that make important decisions without regard or responsibility for discovering the facts will be an insane group and may eventually succumb.

As a leader you should discover your own own facts and do your own research, just as it's always a good practice for any CEO to know and follow up on accounting or legal advice. One should always cross check and verify facts given to one, especially in matters of high importance, before acting upon them as well. Only in this way can you retain your own certainty and confidence, as well as respect from others.

Know History

"The more that you read, the more things you will know. The more that you learn, the more places you'll go."

~ Dr. Seuss

There is no greater resource for a leader than to explore the historical paths others have taken in similar circumstances to one's own. History is a wide open resource for anyone who endeavors to lead others, as it prepares one for predictable outcomes when certain paths are taken.

Make it a key task to study history as it relates to your role in present time. One should not just study the history of the organization one is in (although this, too, is important). One should expand beyond one's own immediate company or organization, and seek to learn the history of similar organizations both contemporary and ancient. Cultures and civilizations have come and gone, but the decisions of their leaders are often recorded and offer insight into outcomes and benefit of knowledge from the paths they have chosen. One can then draw a comparison and gain insight into probable outcomes one could expect from similar decisions others have made.

In this way, history can serve a leader as a rich river of knowledge and wisdom. No one enjoys being in a position where they are compelled to make an important decision blindly, and thus having an understanding of paths others have chosen can benefit and strengthen one's own decision making skills in the journey of leadership.

Tools for Effective Planning

"Men make history and not the other way around. In periods where there is no leadership, society stands still. Progress occurs when courageous, skillful leaders seize the opportunity to change things for the better."

~Harry S. Truman

When taking to task the job of planning for any company or organization, it is always helpful to start with a set of already researched models that have proven to be successful. Being in a position of leadership does not require one to reinvent the wheel with every new challenge one faces. One can also seek out the templates successful organizations have used to build their planning upon.

With this in mind, in 1995 I founded a company called *Shere Strategy Enterprises* (**www.shere-enterprises.com**) to assist people in leadership positions from around the world to start with a solid foundation.

I developed a core trademark concept that Shere Strategy Enterprises uses to do corporate planning work entitled: *The Geometric Cognition Paradigm*.

The Geometric Cognition Paradigm consists of a structured foundation complete with solutions packages designed to address the immediate needs of people in leadership positions as well as clients and organizations they represent. It also addresses and contemplates the many collateral issues directly connected to an initial challenge.

The result is a homogeneous strategy package that provides a comprehensive efficient solution for competitive needs of executives. The company consists of a broad team of strategists, industry professionals and problem-solvers who are success oriented individuals with the skills to guide and strengthen those in positions of leadership.

As a reader of this book, should you wish to find out more about *Shere Strategy Enterprises* and the resources we have available to people in positions of leadership, call (401) 441-1134 or *Info@Shere-Enterprises.com* to arrange for a free consultation with a skilled member of our team with no obligation.

Chapter Five:
Wisdom & Intelligence

"For wisdom is better than rubies, and all the things one may desire cannot be compared with her."

~Proverbs 8:11

There is an important datum that all leaders should understand: *wisdom far outweighs intelligence.* The scriptures in the book of Proverbs offer valuable wisdom for people in a position of leadership. In fact they provide valuable wisdom for anyone.

Intelligence could be said to be the ability to learn and solve problems. Wisdom is the ability to take all that one knows and extrapolate to solve or understand a concept or problem that eludes most people. Wisdom allows the leader to almost predict the future and have sound good judgment to guide his followers through critical times of danger.

I have found through experience that all people who were filled with great wisdom are intelligent, but the reverse is not always true. *All intelligent people are not always wise.*

Always seek wisdom for your endeavors and self-improvement. Solomon, the wisest person to ever live was given a choice by God to have a gift bestowed upon him. He did not choose wealth or power or riches. He chose to have great wisdom. I suppose he realized that with great wisdom he could obtain anything else that he wanted.

The book of proverbs has many great lessons for leaders to benefit from if one examines them. Here are a few examples:

Proverbs 6:27 states *"Can a man scoop fire into his lap without his clothes being burned?"* This Proverb as making a reference to adultery as being the fire one scoops into one's lap, it being plain to see that such actions will have bad effect later if one engages in such behavior. This same piece of wisdom can extend to most any foolish mistake one takes against better judgment, and it is the fool who believes that irresponsible behavior will not burn or scald one later. A potent lesson for anyone in a position of leadership to consider.

Proverbs 26:11 reads: *"As a dog returns to his own vomit, so a fool repeats his folly."* Although upon immediate inspection this sentence may appear somewhat graphic, the wisdom it imparts is profound. Making a mistake and not learning from it, and then repeating it again is not sensible leadership; however one can see the folly by simply observing members of our government and actions of other forms of leadership in society to see that the lesson in this Proverb has not been learned.

Proverbs 13:20 reads: *"Keep company with the wise and you will become wise. If you make friends with stupid people, you will be ruined."* This is a slice of wisdom that so many people could benefit from. Have you ever observed previously brilliant children who later surround themselves with a certain group of friends, and suddenly their own morals fall out? I am sure if you reflect on your experiences, you can probably come up with many examples of this. In the role of leadership, one flourishes and prospers when one surrounds themselves with wise advisors.

There is much to be learned from Proverbs and other ancient books of wisdom. There can be a wealth of information to be had if one takes time to read and study and understand the lessons shared by the wise that have gone before us.

Give Thanks, Be Giving & Share Wisdom

"If you would not be forgotten, as soon as you are dead and rotten, either write things worth reading, or do things worth the writing."

~Benjamin Franklin

When one experiences success in leadership, it is important to remember to give thanks to those who helped you achieve your goals. This is an essential ingredient to continued success.

When one experiences times of plenty and sudden prosperity from success, it is important to also remember to be giving. One should give to charities, people in need and also other groups that are doing good things that need help with financial support.

Likewise, when one benefits from success it is always wise to share that success with others. One way to do this is to share wisdom one has learned with those who are willing to listen. The sharing of wisdom is somewhat akin to the passing along of jewels and treasure to others, however wisdom is far more valuable than material things as it transcends time, especially when it passes along from generation to generation.

Be specific to Your Environment

"If your actions inspire others to dream more, learn more, do more and become more, you are a leader."

~John Quincy Adams

When one is reading books and attempting to apply this new knowledge to a group, it is important to adapt the material learned to be specific to your environment. Taking a raw piece of wisdom from an ancient text and dumping it upon a group in the 20th century, and saying to them *"Okay, just read that and use it"* may or may not have the successful outcome one is looking for.

Taking knowledge and material and making it specific to the environment one is working with is essential. To do otherwise one may defeat one's purpose. One ventures forth to find knowledge so that it can be applied and the golden nuggets one finds can be used. However, if one does not take the time to make sure that those nuggets of wisdom can be understood by everyone else who have not had the opportunity to read and study the background material as you have, it can be a disappointing letdown.

An enthusiastic leader can discover a beautiful nugget of wisdom, and thrust it upon a group only to find they are disheartened and don't embrace the nugget of wisdom with the same vigor.

As an example, let us suppose you discovered a quote from a famous author such as Robert Frost and you found an inspirational quote by him that read *"The best way out is always through".*

One day in a meeting you drop this quote upon the group, without any discussion and wait see how excited they get, and they look at you as if you had said nothing magical, and you are subsequently filled with disappointment.

A good leader would take a different approach: When presenting the quote to the group, he might ask them to discuss how it applies to what they are doing. In this discussion someone might come to a realization *"Oh, you know to me it means finish that job I was working on before I leave for the night"* and another might say *"It means don't give up if you face some difficulty at first"*.

Then the members of the group themselves will begin to take this piece of inspirational wisdom and have further discussion, as they adapt this new wisdom to their understanding and it begins to become something specific to their environment. Once it is specific to their environment, they will see use in it and begin applying it as needed.

Know Your Mission, Know Yourself

"Not the cry, but the flight of a wild duck, leads the flock to fly and follow."

~ Chinese Proverb

As a leader, one must know where he or she intends to lead the group. It is important to have a goal regarding what one wants to achieve.

Without it, one is just drifting along without direction.

The same goes for the understanding one has of one's own self. Never buy into the idea that you are somehow limited in your skill. Never believe that you are inferior, incapable or have reached a ceiling. One can always do better. One can always grow more, and learn more. It is only when one stops seeking to know oneself, and know more in life that one can begin to feel limitations.

Life can be an exploration of knowledge driven by the individual. No one else can know you better. Take time to know yourself, improve your skills and reach for new heights and you will always succeed.

The road to wisdom is the continued willingness to always find out more. As long as you hold true to that quest, you will always find new mountains to summit and vistas to explore.

Chapter Six:
Lead from the Front

"It is better to lead from behind and to put others in front, especially when you celebrate victory when nice things occur. You take the front line when there is danger. Then people will appreciate your leadership."

~ Nelson Mandela

When one enters the role of leadership, it is never a task directed from the rear except in moments when one is empowering others to move forward and get things done.

However, it is also important to remember that the people you lead need to see that you are visible, and approachable, or they will not always follow.

I have always been a firm believer that one should always let the troops see that you as a leader are in front, and when it comes time for events that one should eat last. They will see that you consider that are a leader who is real to them, and at the same time one who is less concerned about yourself and more concerned about success of the group.

It may seem like a subtle message, but it is one that rings true and clear and sets a good example. Those who follow want to have a strong leader. They want their leader to be versatile. They expect you to be compassionate when called for, strong and direct when needed, and confident at all times.

A great leader will give credit to his followers and praise them for the work they do. In the midst of a crisis, a great leader must be able and willing to lead from the front so that his followers can see this confidence and strength. The leader must bear this burden to protect his followers.

I recall an instance in starting an organization that would ultimately have profound effects across the city and its region. Early on a confrontation was brewing between a longtime employee and the new structure of the organization.

The implementation team met to discuss the problem and asked who would go forth to speak with the opposition? I was the president of the fledgling organization and immediately said I would speak with the opposing party to this confrontation alone.

I met with the opposition alone and listened to complaints and ridicule. I waited until I had heard everyone's comments and then I offered the facts, the data, and the reasoning for this unpopular decision.

In doing so, I gained the respect of my team, and the opposition by standing in the breach and taking the fire alone while staying true to our convictions and critical path to success.

Most importantly I listened first, only then did I offer the facts which brought clarity. By listening first, I was able to present the facts and bring about closure on the disagreements being voiced.

People respect the truth, even when it is not in their best interest. As they say, the truth shall set you free. Any leader facing difficult times and confrontation should cling close to the truth, for it will guide one through those difficult times and you will gain the respect of both one's own followers and any opposition.

Be Strong: The Professional Rock

"The final test of a leader is that he leaves behind him in other men, the conviction and the will to carry on."

~ Walter Lippman

I once had taken on a consulting position to lead a struggling organization through a difficult time. I was doing crisis management and several partner organizations became aware of the difficulties facing the organization I was helping.

One day, I met the head of one of the partner organizations who was excited to meet me. She came forward and introduced herself, and mentioned that she previously had heard about my prior work and success with other organizations to help save them from closing their doors. She stated she was very happy that I was helping this struggling organization during this time.

She then asked *"How can you stand in the breach of so much chaos and risk?"* I thought about it briefly and replied *"That's what I do. I go where I am needed."*

She looked at me and said with a smile, *"So you are a Professional Rock?!! Thank you for being here!"* She later mentioned that employees from my organization told her that they felt safer and more secure because of the strength and confidence I displayed, coupled with a calm demeanor and critical thinking to offer concrete solutions to the problems at hand.

What is the lesson in all of this? It is simple: *you must become the Professional Rock for your followers.* Be a steady and strong presence for them to hold onto in times of uncertainty, fear and chaos. Show them true stability and leadership. Exude confidence outwardly, even if inwardly you feel otherwise.

Sometimes leadership is demonstrated by just offering a calm and stable presence in a time of great panic and uncertainty. Exuding confidence and demonstrating control in all that you do, in all the actions you take will not only bring about peace and harmony, it will be infectious and others will soon begin to act the same way over time.

When this occurs, the crisis will soon pass. It is only a stable and confident leader that can put out the fires of raging chaos.

Chapter Seven:
The Heart of the Matter

"To handle yourself, use your head; to handle others, use your heart."

~ Eleanor Roosevelt

When a leader reaches that special place in the guidance of others where his or her motivations, tactics and vision all come into alignment at a spiritual and compassionate level, he has achieved a very special harmony. Success comes when one arrives there, right in the heart.

The Love of People

"Do what you feel in your heart to be right–for you'll be criticized anyway."

~ Eleanor Roosevelt

When I was in my early 20s I had the great opportunity to work and serve people as an Emergency Medical Technician (EMT) in Philadelphia, Pennsylvania. During the time I worked in this job, I had many experiences that gave me a chance to see people at their best doing heroic deeds. Likewise, I saw and experienced people at their worst, displaying acts of profound sadness and basal instincts.

One instance that comes to mind occurred on a rainy evening when my crew and I were dispatched on a call. When you went on a call as an EMT you might have some familiarity with the part of town you were called to, but you never knew exactly what you were walking into. The information given to you by the dispatcher was usually very sketchy or inaccurate. You would have to use your wits to figure out exactly what was happening once you arrived on the scene.

On this particular evening we went to an address and knocked on the door but there was no answer. The dispatcher informed us that he was in contact with an elderly woman's son who lived around the corner and was on his way to the house to meet us. We waited cautiously; being very alert to potential robbery or ambush because unscrupulous people knew EMT vehicles carried drugs that they might be able to use, and some were known to use any means to get at them.

After we had waited for a time in our van, I saw in the rearview mirror a large man sauntering down the street in sort of a loping gait. He started to approach the ambulance and we got out. He then identified himself as the woman's son who had called.

He appeared to be unarmed, so our concerns about robbery subsided. He proceeded to unlock the door to his mother's house so that we could get in. When we entered the house it was quite obvious it was in ill repair. The paint in the hallway was hanging in strips and worn from years of neglect.

We proceeded to follow this man down a narrow hallway. Over our heads swung one naked light bulb from a cathedral ceiling approximately 15 feet above. This limited light lit the downstairs living room and revealed a shadowy narrow winding staircase which appeared to be in a hazardous condition proceeding upwards.

At first I was reluctant to proceed upstairs, assuming the man's mother would be in an upstairs bedroom. I turned to him and asked him where she was, and he pointed to a side room off of the downstairs entrance. Somewhat relieved, we headed in that direction instead.

We came upon a room, and peering into the darkness, there was what appeared to be a figure lying on the sofa. I could just make out the outlines of a person. Throughout the downstairs and as we entered the room, was a combined pungent musty smell and horrific piercing odor of rotting flesh.

I was the senior EMT on duty that evening assigned with a young partner, who instantly began to cover his mouth and his face. I walked closer to the sofa expecting that the woman was deceased and in a state of decomposition. As I got closer, however, I could see that she was indeed breathing.

Initially I thought there was a shadow across her face, but in truth a flashlight revealed it was really her exposed sinus cavity. The flesh had corroded and rotted away so that I could see the roots of her teeth and into the exposed sinus cavities on the front of her face. This woman was in serious need of medical attention.

By some miracle, she was still alive. I asked the son what had happened to her and he said she had fallen a week ago and had been lying on the sofa since then. He told me he would come by sometimes and give her a cup of coffee now and then. As I listened to his detached lack of concern while he explained this to me, I felt the anger well up inside. *How in good conscience could this man leave his mother lying on the sofa in this condition?*

Additionally, she could have been lying there with a fractured hip and most likely had been in excruciating pain for a week or more! Clearly she had defecated and urinated on herself throughout those days, not to mention only surviving on a couple of cups of coffee periodically from this so called son of hers.

However much I wanted to fly into a rage, I controlled my anger and subdued my passion to lash out. My young partner refused to touch her at first, and wanted to leave. I took him on aside and asked him to just do it. He resisted, but I appealed to him by saying that I was determined to take this woman to the hospital, explaining that I would want someone to take my mother if the situation was reversed.

After several minutes urging him to consider the situation from that perspective, he agreed to help me and we picked her up and placed her on the stretcher. We quickly drove her to the hospital emergency room.

After we explained the situation to the emergency room personnel and cleaned ourselves and our stretcher, we were preparing to leave and make ourselves available for the next call. We had just loaded our ambulance and were about to drive off when a nurse came out of the emergency room and stopped us.

He said *"You guys are done for the night"*. I asked what he was talking about since our shift and just started, and we had hours to go before it ended. He explained that once they started to remove the old woman's clothes thousands of lice jumped off of her and into the emergency room.

The result was that both my partner and I, and our ambulance were out of commission for the rest of the night while we were subjected to a delousing process. The emergency room staff had to do the same.

About two months later during a call to a rehabilitation facility I saw the old woman sitting in a chair. I almost did not recognize her, as she had undergone reconstructive surgery on her face and was now getting good care in a nursing home. The nurses there explained that she was doing well. I felt my heart swell with warmth and relief.

When I look back on that experience, to this day I am happy that I was able to convince my partner to help me take her to the hospital. I think about all the other possibilities of that evening as well. *What may have happened if I had lost my temper with her son?* I believe she would've died on the sofa in her own filth.

The lesson in this is that many times a leader must subdue his own passions and emotions to accomplish the task at hand for the betterment of everyone involved. You must put yourself in the other person's shoes and appeal to their emotions, as I did with my young partner, to move forward to accomplish your mission. Most importantly, one must learn to assume leadership and go straight in the heart with your determination.

Let Compassion Be Your Guide

"Leadership cannot just go along to get along. Leadership must meet the moral challenge of the day."

~Jesse Jackson

Another similar incident happened during this time while I was working as an EMT. I was called to a housing project on another vague emergency call. When we arrived there was a crowd at the address with approximately 40 people milling around.

When one is an EMT, there is a tendency to dismiss or ignore comments from members of a crowd at an emergency scene, and take them with a grain of salt because people were untrained.

One woman emerged from the crowd and said she was a neighbor who was caring for an elderly woman. She told me the woman was ill, and just needed some pills, or a bandage, etc. Knowing what I mentioned before about feedback from a crowd, I noted this and asked her to take me to the woman in need of help.

This woman led us into the house to which we were called. Inside there was a sweet elderly sitting in a wheelchair in the middle of a vacant room. The only furniture was a folding card table with lots of mail (mostly bills) piled on top of it.

She was very friendly, smiling and genuinely happy to see us. She looked at me and said *"Hello young man did you come to visit me?"*

I responded *"Yes mother I came to visit you. They told me you didn't feel too good?"*

She replied *"Oh, I feel fine! I just hurt my leg."*

I asked her what happened and she said she had bumped it a few days ago. I asked if I could take a look at it and she said yes, so I got on my knees and lifted her dress up to her knee so that I could examine her shin.

What I saw to my utter shock was hundreds of maggots eating the dead flesh on her shin. I could see through an oval shaped 8 inch hole, the bones of her leg, which were white from where the maggots had been hard at work. This was no minor laceration; it was going to require surgery.

She had no pain, and did not feel a thing. I felt an almost overwhelming empathy for this woman, but also a profound sadness for our elderly who were left to fend for themselves after a lifetime of work.

Without alarming her, I told her that I would take care of her. I put her on a stretcher, and transported her to the hospital. When she arrived at the emergency room, the personnel there fell in love with her and she received very good care.

A few months later I saw her in the rehabilitation center and she had received reconstructive surgery on her leg. Her demeanor was still smiling and sweet.

I learned from this experience that not everything is always as it seems, or is reported by others, and that one needs to look for oneself to find out the condition of things. This is a valuable lesson in leadership. Had I not taken time to really look at what was ailing the patient, and taken what was verbally told to me at the scene, I would have made a tremendous mistake that would have gravely impacted the survival of this woman.

Leadership can come at *anytime*, and take *any form*

"There are three essentials to leadership: humility, clarity and courage."

~Fuchan Yuan

Years later I was traveling in East Africa with a group Americans and some people from various other countries: Great Britain, France, Australia, Germany and Italy. Our group had hired a local driver to take us across the island of Zanzibar, off the coast of Tanzania, in his four-wheel-drive truck.

We all piled into the truck along with our gear. Those that could not fit in the cab climbed into the back of the canopy-covered cargo bed, sandwiched among our gear and supplies. Although we were in no hurry, the driver insisted on speeding down the back country roads despite my requests for him to slow down.

As we approached a precarious curve on a gravel road several dozen miles into the back country, he lost control of the vehicle. I was seated in the front cabin with the driver and remember to this day the feeling of the truck beginning to fishtail uncontrollably, as it proceeded to tip over as if in slow motion.

It all happened so fast. I had time to brace myself, but my hand was hanging outside the window because there were so many of us crowded into the vehicle.

The truck did a complete barrel roll as it slid in circles and bounced along the gravel road before finally coming to a stop as it flipped back onto the wheels again. My hand was caught on the roof of the truck when the rollover occurred, with the result of my hand grinding along the gravel road. I remember thoughts of waiting for my fingers to come off when it all happened.

The truck was destroyed, although upright. I climbed out of the mangled truck window frame and standing shakily upon the gravel road, looked and saw the bodies of my companions scattered along its length. Those who had been in the back of the truck had been strewn in every direction. Some were lying still and not moving.

As I oriented myself for a moment, I could quickly see we were in the middle of nowhere on an unmarked, rural dirt road with no apparent help for miles. My first thoughts racing through my head was that some of these people are dead! *How far is help? What will we do?*

Then I remembered the words of my emergency medical technician instructor, Otto back from my training school. In one of his instruction sessions, he drilled us on what to do at the scene of a disaster. He told us that our training would come back to us in emergency situations, and we would not fail. He said that the first thing you should do upon coming upon the scene of a disaster with multiple fatalities and limited resources was to take one moment, place your right hand on the fender of your ambulance, take a deep breath, and say: *"Oh my God!"*

He described that as our own personal "Oh my God moment" and urged us to take that moment to compose ourselves before beginning the work of saving lives.

Otto was right. As I stood there in the middle of nowhere surrounded by complete chaos, I put my hand on the fender of the mangled truck and looked at my companions along the road and said to myself: *"Oh my God!"*

Immediately all of my emergency management training kicked in and I got into action with doing immediate triage on all the people who were injured. I ignored the injury to my hand, although I knew it was crushed. I could not afford the distraction despite having glanced at it and seeing the exposed bone and blood.

I focused on the task at hand. I worked on assessing the condition of the others, one by one. By a miracle of God's blessings, no one was dead.

However, several had received serious critical injuries.

I started to treat them one by one, wrapping injuries with whatever fabric that would serve for bandaging with what I could find. I cut short sleeves and pant legs, and grabbed laundry from luggage bags tossed along the road.

I made a structure out of the canopy in the back of the truck, and created neck braces out of towels to stabilize fractured backs. I gave mouth-to-mouth for people who were in respiratory distress, and did all the things an EMT is trained to do without all of the resources of an ambulance.

The driver, who had been very rude earlier while driving, was now frantically apologizing to me. He somehow survived without injury. I ignored him, and just wanted him to get out of my way. I was tempted to punch him, but I focused on treating the injured people and merely ignored him.

People from a nearby village after a time arrived to help and I directed them on how to assist me in caring for the injured. At one point, I saw that the driver had walked down the road a few hundred yards and fainted. Looking back, I remember considering this to be one of the oddest surreal things to witness. Even more unbelievable was that the people from the village literally stepped over his body in the middle of the road and didn't try to help him at all.

Eventually another vehicle arrived coming along the same road, which I considered to be yet another miracle. The villagers stopped him and the driver helped us to load all of the injured into his vehicle and he drove us to a field hospital.

This "field hospital" we arrived at was nothing more than a makeshift compound with dirt floors and chickens running around. I soon discovered that my EMT training was superior to the doctors who were in training at this place. I used a blood pressure cuff to take some vital signs of my injured companions, and stabilized their injuries as best that I could.

Fortunately this facility had a working telephone where I was able to call the embassy and ask for help. They also had a jeep which enabled us to drive all the injured to the city of Zanzibar arriving at a more adequate temporary hospital facility.

I found I was in-charge, by default or as fate would have it. I had assumed a leadership role unexpectedly, and I was in control. I arranged for my companions treatments.

Soon caring people who were expatriates heard that there were Americans at the hospital and came to our aid. They used their connections to make arrangements for medical flights from the island back to Nairobi hospital in Kenya, which was one of the best hospitals in Africa.

While waiting for our transport to Nairobi in the facility in Zanzibar after everyone had been treated, I found myself sitting exhausted on the edge of a bench when a doctor was walking by. Another patient stopped him as he passed and pointed at my hand, which have not been treated in all of the day long events. In fact, when my training had kicked in out in the back country, I had successfully tuned out the pain as adrenaline took over.

The doctor couldn't believe it and he said to me: *"I thought you were helping them, but I didn't know you were a patient and injured as well!"*

He immediately took me aside, and cleaned my wounds, bandaged my hand securing splints to my broken fingers. At one point he asked me if I wanted something for the pain, but I refused because I wanted to be alert for anything we needed to do for our evacuation to Nairobi. I was still focused on my leadership role I had assumed, and was dedicated to the care of my fellows.

The expatriates stayed with us, but they continued to ask me over and over again: *What happened to the driver?* I thought this was very curious, and did not understand their interest. I finally inquired, and one of them explained to me that in this part of Africa there is usually mob justice at the scene of an accident where the mob will quite often kill the driver.

This immediately explained to me why the villagers had stepped over the driver's body in the middle of the road, giving him no attention. I caught my breath, and said a prayer to myself thanking God that I had not punched the man when I wanted to. I now understood if I had done so, it may have ignited a spark of a mob justice killing right there at the scene. I hoped that my restraint at that moment had somehow saved the man from such a fate, but I will never know.

My ex-patriot friends made arrangements to open the airport at night, which normally closed after dark. A warm sigh of relief passed over me when I could hear the plane coming in to land on the runway. A short time later, we were safely flown to the Nairobi hospital, and everyone survived.

I am forever reminded that leadership comes in many forms, at any time, for anyone. We must marshal all of our experience, knowledge, strength, and insights to address the challenges before us and also be prepared to accept help from others when one is in charge. The lessons in this experience were many, but perhaps the most important is that when one is following their heart in times of chaos, it is the best guide of all. It is right in the heart of the matter.

The Compassion Project

"If it is not tempered by compassion, and empathy, reason can lead men and women into a moral void."

~ Karen Armstrong,
Twelve Steps to a Compassionate Life

The book *"Twelve Steps to a Compassionate Life"* by Karen Armstrong is a guide to help leaders and people of all walks of life to build a more compassionate world together. I serve on a committee for an organization that has adopted those principles from her book to convey into the community at large in whatever capacity we leaders can facilitate.

Karen Armstrong won the coveted TED prize in 2008(An award for extraordinary individuals with a creative and bold vision to spark global change) for her work in this field of building compassion around the world. This work sparked a movement with religious leaders from many faiths to create a universal 'Charter for Compassion' which called for the restoration of compassion to the heart of a religious and moral life in a dangerously polarized world.

Within this movement to forward the ideas in her book, people are urged everywhere to sign a petition for this Charter for Compassion which gets forwarded to leaders in our communities and the municipal state and federal government.

Armstrong's book examines our aggressive attitudes toward each other as a result of the actions of the reptilian brain and our search for basic needs, food, shelter, sex, recognition and comfort.

A great leader inherently loves his followers. That is why a leader will take on the burden and role of leadership and are willing to make many personal sacrifices for the greater good. I would encourage all leaders of any organization or group of people who guide a church, government, family, corporation, or any volunteer efforts, to read her book and do their best to adopt those principles. They are a guide for not only understanding compassion, but one for great leadership.

People as a rule are not stupid. In fact they are very smart and observant. They can tell when someone is sincere or not. Followers will be able to tell whether you sincerely care about their well-being and safety and security, or whether you are a phony.

Babies and children can tell someone's heart. We all know people around us who invoke smiles and laughter from children and babies. Scientific studies tell us the children and babies can read the facial expressions of adults and have an innate ability to sense sincerity.

As we get older we start to rationalize and cloud our intuition with intellectual thoughts, but we do retain that ability to read facial expressions and detect a gut level of sincerity from other people. You must truly and honestly love your followers, and sincerely have genuine compassion to be an effective leader. The people who follow you can tell if you are sincere, or not.

Having a love for your followers equips you as a leader with great strength and fortitude. This will enable you to overcome many obstacles and face any hardships thrust upon you. It is the path to becoming a great leader.

Chapter Eight:
Being a Visionary

"Where there is no vision, the people perish"

~ Proverbs 29:18

To be a leader, one must be able to envision the future. To do this, all great leaders establish goals for the organization they are leading and lay out where they want to go. That constitutes the overall vision of the future.

Overarching Goals & Lower Goals

"Nothing can stop the man with the right mental attitude from achieving his goal; nothing on earth can help the man with the wrong mental attitude."

~ Thomas Jefferson

When acting in a position of leadership, one must remember that there are different goals of various sizes for every organization. There can be many small goals, but usually there are one or two significant 'overarching' goals. An *overarching goal* could best be defined as: *A goal that overshadows all other goals.*

People with whom I have worked on major projects have credited me with an ability to *"cut to the chase"* and get to the heart of the matter when tackling projects. What I have discovered is that when people discuss a problem or obstacle or challenge, often they cloud the issue. I believe the best way to remove the cloud from the issue, is to focus on your goals, especially the overarching ones.

Too often we lose track of our goal and get sidetracked with collateral issues. Focus on your goals, starting with the overarching goals. From there, it makes it much easier to identify a critical path to success.

If your plan of action is stalling or not progressing, ask yourself: *Are your actions leading on a clear path to your goal or is it a collateral issue?* Keep only those actions which will take you to your goal, and discard the rest.

You may have several objectives that work simultaneously toward the overarching goal, and this is where a group effort may get sidetracked. But the same principle remains true. Even though there may be multiple objectives, one should still keep the overarching goal in mind.

For example, your goal may be to save an organization from closing, but that goal will encompass many lower level objectives as well, such as a public relations plan, a financial and fiscal plan and an organizational assessment which may result in personnel changes. Each segment for meeting your objectives must move along the critical path for successfully reaching your overarching goals.

Here is an illustration of the above example:

If one looks at this graphic, it is easy to see that the overarching goal has many parts that are essential to it being successfully accomplished. If one attempts to save the company from closing, but omits to address some form of reorganization to avoid falling back into the same operating basis that got the company in trouble to begin with, the overarching goal can never be accomplished.

Likewise, if a public relations plan is not implemented, one may never recover old customers who left or repair the image the company may have suffered from its previous decline. Do you see how they are all connected?

There can be many lower level goals, and quite often they outnumber the primary or overarching goals. They are the smaller parts to the whole solution, and all are integral to the others success.

Achieving the Impossible

"If you took one-tenth the energy you put into complaining and applied it to solving the problem, you'd be surprised by how well things can work out... Complaining does not work as a strategy. We all have finite time and energy. Any

time we spend whining is unlikely to help us achieve our goals. And it won't make us happier."

~ Randy Pausch, *The Last Lecture*

When faced with a challenging situation or task, I love to hear someone tell me, *"That's impossible. It can't be done".*

That type of statement motivates me and inspires me to do the impossible. I often say to a new team I begin working with the following: *It is easy to have 10 people tell me the reasons why something cannot be done, but I only find value in the one person who can tell me how it can be done!*

Don't get me wrong and misunderstand this message. A leader should be circumspect and consider the obstacles and challenges to success. However, one must focus on the success and not get bogged down in the challenge and the obstacles.

There are certain ingredients that you need in order to achieve the impossible:

1. *You must believe it can be done.*
2. *You must research the objective and the challenges.*

3. *You must have the personnel to achieve the goal.*

There is a reason why 10 people are telling you it can't be done; listen and understand *why* your team is thinking that way. Then, you must think and approach the situation in a different way.

Think *outside* of the box. Do not compartment your thinking into small ideas and limited goals. Don't get caught up in what has gone before, what others are doing, or any of those things. To solve the impossible, one must think with original ideas and concepts.

Employers these days look for analytical skills in the people they hire. Likewise, a leader must be able to analyze the situation and think in multiple ways from multiple dimensions, and perspectives to overcome obstacles and challenges and find solutions.

Looking at the third point above, you must have the personnel to get the job done. One cannot always do the job alone. Some leaders make the mistake of trying to do the entire job themselves. However, if you are trying to do it all yourself, then there may be a component of your leadership that is lacking. You must know yourself, and know who you need to help achieve your star-high goals. Identify those people and bring them into your circle and get them on your team.

Knowing Oneself & Know your People

"Knowing yourself is the beginning of all wisdom."

~ Aristotle

Knowing oneself is an integral part of being a visionary. One must know that one can accomplish a goal one sets out to achieve, but one must also know that the bigger the goal, the more help will be needed to make it a reality.

Being a visionary does not mean one acts alone. On the contrary, one learns that a successful leader leads, and gets others to do, and thus arrives at the accomplished goal.

So know yourself, and know your people. Achieve the impossible, and conquer your goals!

Chapter Nine:
Overcoming Obstacles & Pitfalls

"The lotus is the most beautiful flower, whose petals open one by one. But it will only grow in the mud. In order to grow and gain wisdom, first you must have the mud --- the obstacles of life and its suffering. ... The mud speaks of the common ground that humans share, no matter what our stations in life. ... Whether we have it all or we have nothing, we are all faced with the same obstacles: sadness, loss, illness, dying and death. If we are to strive as human beings to gain more wisdom, more kindness and more compassion, we must have the intention to grow as a lotus and open each petal one by one. "

~Goldie Hawn

"Aut inveniam viam aut faciam" is the Latin phrase for "I will either find a way.... *or make one!"* I first heard this quote in college and have since then incorporated it into my life. This

phrase has become one of my favorite personal mottos. I live by those words.

Whenever I am confronted with a challenge of seemingly insurmountable magnitude, I hear this motto in my head. It has been attributed to Hannibal. Benjamin Franklin used it often.

A great leader must adopt this attitude as he or she will inevitably be faced with daunting challenges that must be faced head-on, and failure is never an option. Use all of your emotional, physical, spiritual, intellectual and material resources to extrapolate using synergy to find solutions and achieve the impossible.

In previous chapters, we have already mentioned that there are pitfalls and unforeseen circumstances that any leader faces. There are specific pitfalls for any effort that a person is trying to navigate. You as the leader must identify the specific pitfalls to which your effort may be subject, preferably before they are encountered.

The leader can also be the subject to personal pitfalls. Sometimes our own ideas and counter ideas can be the source of a lot of entanglements. I find that adhering to the principles of love, specifically true love for one's followers, and a real commitment to compassion will help to avoid many of the personal pitfalls to which leaders may succumb.

Temptations

"Temptation is the devil looking through the keyhole. Yielding is opening the door and inviting him in."
~Billy Sunday

The media is replete with stories of political, religious and civic leaders having extramarital affairs, or inappropriate sexual exploits that destroy their leadership and profoundly affect the noble efforts which they undertook. Nothing can destroy the foundation of a leader faster than a scandal. The best way to prevent a scandal is to not place oneself in a position to create one.

A leader must understand that the mantle of leadership is an attraction to many people. The leader must not succumb to the temptation of having an affair with a follower. This is not to say that a leader may not fall in love with the following, but don't mistake true love and a meaningful long-term relationship with a fling that will ultimately hurt one's followers and one's reputation.

Again, if the leader is looking at true love for his followers and compassion he can avoid making this mistake. Leadership means being strong enough to rise above one's own personal desires and interests, and maintain a personal standard of integrity that is above such temptation.

This does not mean one cannot have a personal life, it means that this type of personal life and the business of leading are two lines that should never cross if one is to maintain a stable position of leadership.

Be willing and able to listen

"The spoken word belongs half to him who speaks, and half to him who listens."

~French Proverb

Another temptation the leaders may succumb to that can be destructive is *arrogance.* A great leader must be conscientious and able to really listen. Listening is at the top of the list of qualities for a great leader. There is a proverb that says: *one should use his ears and his mouth in that proportion.*

In other words listen two thirds of the time in any conversation. Use compassion and love when addressing those you lead and place yourself in their shoes and position. The person who can put himself in other people's shoes has great power. He or she will be able to empathize and find solutions that will pull people together in a group effort and inspire them to overcome obstacles and achieve the impossible.

Another thing leaders should be aware of is to not talk just for the sake of talking. Your people want to hear how you will lead them to success. Time is a valuable commodity and no one wants to feel like they have wasted it. A great leader will gain lots of support by showing people the path to success. You must connect the dots for people you lead by showing them the goal, the path, and how you will get there. It must be obtainable and understandable. In this manner, people are much more ready to follow you and a clear plan down a pathway to success.

The Concept of the Enemy

"Do I not destroy my enemies when I make them my friends?"

~ Abraham Lincoln

There is no such thing as an enemy. Certainly, this will take some convincing in some people. What is an enemy really? It is a person with a contrary or opposing viewpoint or opposition to your own. It is a force counter to your force, but it does not necessarily make that person evil. Does man act evil at times? Most certainly he does.

Crimes and criminals occur daily in some places. This does not dismiss that notion. This statement is only clarifying that the concept of the enemy is something created by a culture of fear. Fear creates the enemy, real or imagined.

To believe there are enemies, one must be driven by fear. True leaders must be fearless; therefore to overcome the obstacle of fear, one must assume the position that there are no enemies.

Are there misguided people? Crazy people? Scary people? Most certainly there are all of those. However, these are mostly moral and ethical qualities, and it does not necessarily make them an *enemy*.

One person is driving for a goal in one direction and the other in another, and they encounter each other in apparent conflict to each other's purposes, and thus they assign each other the title of 'enemy'. Enemies are most often created from a communication breakdown of some sort.

Sometimes one takes action against the other, fueling the foundation of a bad relationship and this further compounds the problem. However, even this can be resolved and calm waters can prevail with good communication eventually.

Not everyone will always agree with you or your goals. This does not make them your enemy. It means you need to choose a better circle of people on your team. As mentioned earlier in Proverbs 13:20: *"Keep company with the wise and you will become wise."*

There perhaps were no truer words ever written about the type of people one should seek to be surrounded by. People of contrary viewpoint to your own are not the ones you need to bring close to your planning circle. They will not help you reach your goals, and you will be tempted into conflict or deem them your enemy, which serves no purpose. Find team members of similar purpose and who are willing to follow similar goals, and you will have no enemies.

Rachel: The Story & the Lesson

"The challenge of leadership is to be strong, but not rude; be kind, but not weak; be bold, but not bully; be thoughtful, but not lazy; be humble, but not timid; be proud, but not arrogant; have humor, but without folly."

~Jim Rohn

There was a girl that I met only briefly once, and I still think of her often. I sometimes reflect on her while working at my desk, or when watching my children play. Sometimes at night when I look at the night sky I think of her. Her name is Rachel, and she was beautiful. She was one of those special people that come into your life and touch you in a way that changes you forever.

I met her one night when I was an Emergency Medical Technician (EMT) in Philadelphia. It was later in my career in that profession, when I was part of a select team of professionals who were trained and trusted with the task of long distance transport of high risk patients on an emergency basis.

We worked out of some of the trauma centers in the Philadelphia metropolitan area and we would travel throughout Pennsylvania and parts of New Jersey to smaller hospitals and retrieve patients requiring more urgent care. We would retrieve high risk patients, with serious third-degree burns over good portions of their bodies in critical condition and transport them to the burn centers in Philadelphia. We would also retrieve premature babies sometimes weighing less than 1 pound and bring them to the neonatal centers in Philadelphia.

I was proud and happy to belong to this team, which had a reputation for saving many lives and getting them safely to their destinations. During my time with this special EMT team, we held a universal pride that we never had lost a patient. Every one of our missions had been a success, and all of our patients had lived.

When I reflect back on it now, I would have considered myself at that time in my youth somewhat over-confident, cocky and arrogant. Our track record was perfect. We knew it, and we sometimes boasted letting others know it in our circles.

That all changed one evening we got a call to go out to Easton, Pennsylvania, the hometown of heavyweight boxing champion Larry Holmes.

Residents in the town are very proud of the fact that it was Larry Holmes' hometown, and they were quick to let you know whenever they could fit it into a conversation. Upon our arrival at the hospital, a circa 1960s facility, we unloaded our equipment swiftly and charged up the hill entering the lobby and began asking for the location of the emergency patient.

We were directly upstairs which we ascended two and three steps at a time, moving people quickly out of our way, when reaching the top we shot down the hallway. We burst into the trauma unit like rodeo cowboys, announcing ourselves to the staff in charge of the unit. My team and I felt like we were the cavalry there to save the day.

We were directed to the patient's room down a short hallway. We entered and there she was: *Rachel*, a six hours old premature baby girl weighing only 2 ½ pounds. The team and I jumped into an immediate fury of activity and started to work on her. We ran many, many tests. We took vital signs, retesting, and retesting into the night. After a time, we had the answer. Rachel was going to die. Her lungs were not fully developed, and she would not survive.

I watched as her young father was told that his baby was going to die. He cried and looked at me, and I'll never forget this, he said *"Showtime"* and stood straight up pulling his emotions together.

He spun on his heels and walked into his wife's room. He composed himself in an instant to be strong for her as he relayed the heartbreaking news and assured her that they would have other children.

I still marvel at the incredible strength of that young man in the way he put aside his own grief to comfort his wife. The young couple had a terrible decision to make, that no parent should ever have to face.

They could give Rachel to us to transport to Philadelphia, where she would most likely die during the trip, or keep her there with them until she passed away. They chose to keep her with them.

The room felt as if a bomb had been dropped on it. All the members of my team were quiet. All of our bravado and arrogance was swept aside in a fleeting instant. We quietly loaded our equipment back into the ambulance, where we took a long solemn ride back to

Philadelphia in virtual silence. I remember a light rain began to fall. Staring out the passenger window on the ride back I thought I saw raindrops running down the reflection of my face in the glass, but soon I realized it was my own tears.

There are incidents in our lives that can change you forever. That evening, I learned the futility of arrogance and the wisdom of humility. I learned a harsh lesson of death and defeat.

I had seen people die before, but never one that was in my care, and never one so young. Since that day I take solace in three things; my faith in God, my hope that through this story Rachel may live on in our hearts, and lastly, the resilience of our human existence, and hope.

One of the most important lessons one can learn as a leader is humility. It is not something one can read in a text book, or learn in a leadership conference. It is something that has to come deep down from within, in a place within your heart; *right in the heart.*

Hope & Survival

"Losing the possibility of something is the exact same thing as losing hope and without hope

nothing can survive."

~ Mark Z. Danielewski

I find value in governmental studies sometimes. There was one study where they researched, tested and interviewed survivors of disasters. They interviewed plane crash survivors, shipwreck survivors, people who would have been lost at sea, to people who have been subjected to tornados and hurricanes, people who had been firefighters trapped in fires where their comrades died, but they survived. The profile of the people in the study was that they were lone survivors of tragedies.

The researchers wanted to know what was different about them. What enabled them to survive when everyone around them perished? Many of them carried great grief and a sense of guilt that they had survived while their friends or loved ones or even strangers died.

However, the researchers found one common thread. Were they stronger? No, not physically. Were they smarter? Not necessarily by I.Q. testing. Were they just plain lucky? No facts supported this either. Were they prepared? No more than any of the others caught in the disaster.

The common thread for each of the soul survivors was one thing: *They never gave up hope.*

Not a one of them ever believed that they would die in the disaster. No matter how bad the situation got, they fought, they were determined to live and never gave up hope.

In a challenging situation, or tragedy, or disaster, family crisis, or business meltdown, the leader must endeavor to the best of his or her ability to instill a strong sense of hope into his or her followers. Without hope, all is lost. Failure comes when hope exits. You will not survive.

Never, ever give up hope. This is a cornerstone in the foundation of any leader facing a challenging or threatening environment. Never give up hope. Hope rules the day.

Chapter Ten:
Motivation

"Leaders must be close enough to relate to others, but far enough ahead to motivate them."

~John C. Maxwell

In the midst of any great endeavor, at the outset or during hardships along the way, the leader will encounter situations where he must motivate those who follow. If your goal is worthwhile you will inevitably reach points along the way where the people you are leading or yourself may lose momentum and require additional motivation.

The leader must constantly be on the lookout and observant for these instances. Not recognizing a time when further motivation for the group is needed will lead to other problems. One of the keys to motivating people is to place oneself in their shoes and view the situation from multiple perspectives.

Never be judgmental if people are losing motivation. It is an inevitable occurrence that can happen along the way in any journey. *Instead ask yourself why?* And consider what you would do if you too felt that way. *What would make you feel better and more willing to continue the journey? Has it been a long struggle? Does the group need to take a rest? Does the group need to hear encouragement or do they need a reward? Are they afraid?*

When you have the answers to those questions, find the words or materials that can answer those questions and restore confidence in your own efforts. Bring that strength to them.

Understand what Motivates

"A good motivation is what is needed: compassion without dogmatism, without complicated philosophy; just understanding that others are human brothers and sisters and respecting their human rights and dignities. That we humans can help each other is one of our unique human capacities. "

~ Dalai Lama XIV

I once climbed Mount Kilimanjaro, the tallest mountain in Africa which rises to a height of 19341 feet. It is a four-day hike to the top and the climber ascends through a variety of terrains: tropical jungle, savanna, desert, and finally freezing glacier conditions with snow as one approaches the summit.

It is a grueling hike which takes anywhere from four to eight days to complete on average, depending on weather conditions. One must carry every piece of gear needed for survival in a variety of elements and climates on your back, including water and food. There were 19 of us that started the journey, only seven of us made it to the top.

Along the way, I became friends with a man who was making the climbed with his wife. They were both in their 60s, and taking on the challenge together. On day three, the night before we were to make the final ascent to the summit, this gentleman's wife became very ill. Many of the climbers succumb to altitude sickness near the top, and we were approximately at about 18,000 feet at this point in the journey.

The oxygen becomes thin and causes edema and problems across the blood brain barrier. People can become violently ill, with symptoms including vomiting and nausea. The condition can become quite threatening, and there is always a risk of death.

The morning of our final ascent, I was shocked when this gentleman left his wife to take final trip to the summit without her. I was tempted to berate him for leaving her in that condition. Luckily for me, I held my tongue.

When our small group of surviving climbers made it to the top he moved away from the group. He pulled a bundle out of his pack, and I noticed it was an urn. He opened it, said some words softly to himself, and poured ashes onto the ground and into the wind.

On the decent down, he later explained to me that he was determined to make it to the top of Mount Kilimanjaro because his father was born in Tanzania and always wanted to get to the top of the mountain, but had died recently. He wanted to make sure that his father, whose ashes he carried, were spread on top of the mountain.

He was motivated even at the risk of his wife's poor health and well-being for that ideal. Sometimes, we must all ask ourselves what we are willing to do to accomplish a goal.

At times our actions may appear unreasonable to others around us, but we must all examine this for ourselves and truly understand our own personal motivation to achieve a goal. At his age this gentleman risked his own life, and maybe his wife's, to perform this final act of devotion in honor of his father.

The completion of that task was the image he carried in his mind each step of the way up the mountain, and it made it possible for him to summit Kilimanjaro despite all obstacles. It was a goal important to him, his wife and his father. Something he felt worthy of such a risk.

Motivation is essential for any individual to achieve a goal. Without it, at best there is just a meandering or wandering that occurs. Groups that are motivated make progress towards a goal rapidly. Groups that are not often go off in many directions and accomplish nothing. A worthy goal made clear to a group will motivate its members to achieve, even if at great risk.

Chapter Eleven:
The Corporate Mentality

"The best executive is the one who has sense enough to pick good men to do what he wants done, and self-restraint enough to keep from meddling with them while they do it."

~Theodore Roosevelt

I grew up in a major corporation starting in the Pharmaceutical Industry at the age of 19 years old. Due to this early start, I sometimes refer to myself as a 'Corporate Baby', having spent so many years navigating these waters.

I worked for a Fortune 500 company, which had facilities across the globe. I was given a unique education; what I refer to now as a *corporate education.* It is an insulated world, and I was able to see how many corporations operate on the inside. Each one has its own culture, values, ethics, goals and morality. Each has its own system of rewards.

The leaders of each of these corporations set the tone for all the employees within the organization.

Years later I was impressed when I heard the story of the Southwest Airlines culture. One time I was flying on Southwest and noticed that when my plane landed a different crew came in to clean the plane cabin in preparation for the next flight.

On other airlines on which I had flown, I had always observed that the flight attendants that were on duty cleaned the plane upon landing. I asked one of the Southwest crew about the difference. She smiled and said this was their day off, but they came in to help the attendants on duty so that they may have a break between flights.

It is a practice which is part of the culture of teamwork and camaraderie that they all share. What a wonderful concept, and a group of people that are real team members! I've seen those same efforts and departments in various companies where I have worked, a sense of camaraderie and helping one another.

Some corporations have a profound sense of community citizenship where they earnestly lend assistance to the community in which they are based. Unfortunately, just as with people as individuals, some corporations are self-serving, greedy and downright unethical. Their morality is based upon exploitation, as opposed to their counter-parts that do the opposite.

However difficult, individuals can take the initiative and change the way of thinking and acting of an entire group. This can change the entire division and send ripples of positive behavior throughout the corporation.

Corporations are entities comparable to people. Some are good-natured and some are not. It is the leadership within each that functions as the conscience and moral compass for any given corporation.

Corporations can also act as if they are a sociopath, as depicted in the 2003 Canadian documentary entitled 'The Corporation' which profiled and examined the modern day corporate model. Based on the book written by University of British Colombia law professor Joel Bakan entitled 'The Corporation: Pathological Pursuit of Profit and Power', through vignettes and interviews, this documentary examines and criticizes corporate business practices.

Despite the corporations that do act without the framework of morals, there are ones that have a solid foundation based on honesty and hard work that filters down from their leadership. It is this leadership that sets the tone for the corporation, no matter what its size. This is where leadership can be spotlighted and highlighted for all to see.

Government bureaucracies and non-profit organizations are not immune to this kind of corporate phenomenon, as the larger they grow, the more they too, can resemble an uncaring juggernaut with no conscience.

It is the leaders of any size organization that put the focus on success. This can create a production model based on a good, honest effort. When such an entity is in place, one can see employees at many levels of the organization taking initiative as in the example given with Southwest Airlines above.

People will grow to enjoy being part of the team, and want to help the company grow and prosper, so they will take initiative to make things better and help each other.

So understanding what one can run into with dealing with the corporate mentality is important, but it is even more important to understand that corporations are made up of people.

People can change, and good people can change things for the better. So no matter the size of the corporation or other organization, remember that it is made up of people and they are the most powerful ingredient in the entire formula.

Chapter 12:
'It's good to be King'

"A good leader is a person who takes a little more than his share of the blame and a little less than his share of the credit."

~John Maxwell

In 1981 Mel Brooks released a comedy movie called *"History of the World Part One"* that depicted various stages of human civilization throughout history with a comedic view.

There was one particular segment of the movie featuring King Louis of France, (portrayed by Brooks) among other members of his court. Different events occur around him involving other people suffering from lack of food, injured, afflicted by diseases, war, etc. Brooks would engage in unsavory rude behavior, and then look at the camera and speak to the audience watching him, saying with a smile *"It's good to be the king"*. Wherever he went, and whatever rude behavior or careless conduct, he would pause, look at the camera and repeat the same one line *"It's good to be the king"*, over and over again.

This line became a running joke with people throughout the generation. In fact it became part of the social vernacular. People in leadership positions began using that quote whenever a situation arose where they had privilege above their followers.

This of course was a joke. The reality for true leader is that he or she quite often bears a heavier burden than his followers. He or she is responsible for the entire group. They are often the first to arrive, and the last to leave an organization within the span of daily operation, and often must take their work home with them. They have the task of making sure that their followers are comfortable and safe, as leading is a full time activity.

One must lead from the front in times of trouble and uncertainty, as well as face any hardship. Leaders must be the ones who work harder to find solutions to situations which seem beyond solution. Despite pressures to do otherwise, they must also subdue their own emotions when dealing with rude and hostile followers.

Above all, they must display strength in order to give comfort to their followers, even when they may be hurting. In reality it may not be so good to be the king. However, for the true leader, it is an inescapable responsibility because of the love they have for their followers.

The leader must be able to deal with them whether they are family, a church congregation, co-workers, employees, neighbors, constituents (as in an elected official) or merely strangers brought together in an emergency situation.

Leadership must embrace all who follow, and there can sometimes be no peace or rest. Leadership positions can sometimes be lonely where one is exclusively devoted to the caring of others, that one has no time for oneself. It requires dedication, tenacity and persistence at all times, good or bad.

So on the surface to the casual uninformed observer it may seem to be good to be the king, but more often than not it can be a thankless job with few personal rewards. The rewards are at different levels, it is the success of the group or organization that becomes the high point. It is the struggles and set-backs that become the low points. However it is the journey above all that creates the enduring happiness.

Chapter 13:
Lead by Example

"The key to successful leadership today is influence, not authority."

~Kenneth Blanchard

A leader must be able to set a good example to exemplify good character to his or her people. As discussed in earlier chapters, one's behavior can be more destructive to the integrity of the group than outside influences. How a leader behaves is seen by everyone, particularly by the members of your group.

Setting a good example is therefore a matter that a leader cannot take lightly. People will follow leaders with good moral character, and avoid or undermine ones who lack it. Success lies in being in the former category, and not the latter.

People Watch the Leader

"Command from a forward position, which means from the thick of it. No soldier will ever be inspired to advance into a hail of bullets by orders phoned in on the radio from the safety of a remote command post; he is inspired to follow the officer in front of him. It is much more effective to get your personnel to follow you than to push them forward from behind a desk."

~David Carrison

I've learned one crucial lesson when it comes to leading people. Always keep this in mind: *people are always watching.* People may not say anything for long periods of time, but they are watching everything you do and listening to everything you say. They talk amongst themselves and compare notes. They watch to see if your words match your actions.

I have learned that people will follow if they see someone else do it first. As an example of this, one day I was in a busy commuter train concourse in a large East Coast city at morning rush hour. There were literally thousands of people running to catch the trains to make it to work on time, carrying their coffee, their briefcases and the morning paper. A typical day has everyone concerned about their own agenda in starting their day, and they are focused on getting to their train.

As I was walking across the concourse expanse through this throng of people, I noticed a McDonald's bag of trash on the floor. Scores of people were walking past it and over it. As I approached it I bent down without breaking stride grabbed the bag and continued a few more steps on my course and dropped it in the nearest wastebasket.

I took a few more steps and noticed a man about 20 feet away making eye contact with me as we approached each other. As we got closer, he smiled and he said *"I saw what you did"*. I smiled back and kept walking, but turned to watch him after we had passed.

Without him knowing I was looking, I saw that he also bent down and picked up another bag of trash and threw it in a waste basket on his way to his train.

That experience taught me that each of us as individuals can take on a leadership role by taking that first step. Others are watching our every move, but waiting for someone else to do

what they know is the right thing to do.
Remember there are the 80% of which we speak:
the watchers. By taking simple action for the
greater good, others will emulate that action and
thus we can start the beginnings of a fantastic
movement.

The same concept rings true in
organizations. I've changed the demeanor of an
office by being the first one to bring a box of
donuts and coffee for everyone, offering to help
someone with a project who I knew was
struggling, or cleaning a common area.

Leaders are servants who take the
initiative to serve. *Watchers* will follow along
that same line of service if they see others do it
first.

Leadership Percolates to the Top

*"Leaders aren't born, they are made. And
they are made just like anything else, through hard
work. And that's the price we'll have to pay to
achieve that goal, or any goal."*

~Vince Lombardi

You will be surprised at how a simple
taking of initiative will compel others to emulate

those same actions. Sometimes they feel embarrassed that they did not come up with the idea themselves. The truth is that they have the mindset of the 80%, and so they watch and wait for others first.

One of the key things you will learn by demonstrating caring and effective leadership to others within this 80% is that you will help to bring some of them out of that group, and into the 10% who take initiative and lead.

Leaders are not born leaders, they are made. They sometimes have to be shown how to be a leader, and so therefore watching for many is the first step to becoming a leader themselves.

Leadership positions pull people up from the 80% group, almost as a natural action through the necessity of the situation which demands they step up.

Not everyone answers the call, but there will always be ones that do, and in so doing they percolate into that 10% club of ones who can.

This is how they are created, sometimes through the mold of necessity and timing, but nevertheless they either rise to the challenge or someone near them in the same pool does.

Take Care of Yourself

"People buy into the leader before they buy into the vision."
~John Maxwell

In the course of setting an example, one must also learn to take care of oneself. That means getting rest, eating healthy and exercising regularly.

Putting bad fuel into your body over time will only bring your energy down, and physical energy is necessary sometimes to compel others to action. By taking care of yourself, you show that you care enough to survive a long time and make yourself available to continue to lead.

It shows many things, but overall it sets a good example for others who are watching you. By taking care of yourself as a leader, and knowing others are watching you and will follow what you do, you are in effect saving all the lives of your followers too.

So keep that in mind when you go to the gym next or reach for the salad over the hamburger.

Telling Stories

"But how could you live and have no story to tell?"

~ Fyodor Dostoyevsky

When one is seeking to lead by example, there is no better example one than in the form of a story. Stories have been a means of conveying lessons, important wisdom, potential futures and outcomes and many other concepts for centuries. Instead of telling someone to do something which makes sense to you, tell them a story so that they can see *why it makes sense.*

Use your own experiences, or discover others who offer such stories in books, word of mouth, etc.

Go in search of stories that you can use to illustrate the important points that you wish to teach your followers. This is an age old tool, and it was used by ancient people to relay history through time. It also had the purpose of teaching valuable lessons to others that in essence could not be taught in any other way.

Chapter Fourteen:
Leadership & Relationships

"You don't lead by hitting people over the head—that's assault, not leadership."

~Dwight Eisenhower

If one is to lead others one can scarcely negate the necessity of having good relationships with the people one is working shoulder to shoulder with, as well as the ones one is serving.

I have never been a proponent of pressuring people to do what I want. I never take the position that I know all the elements and aspects or perspectives of a situation or challenge. I will always consider an ally's suggestion or insights, or even their opposing viewpoint.

I believe it is a supreme mistake to impress my will on other people, especially ones who have entrusted me with the mantle of leadership.

Forcing people, threatening them, and or beating your followers into production in one form or another is just abuse. People will not take that indefinitely; soon you will turn and find there is no one left behind you. Leadership is when people want to follow you, not only when they are forced to do what you say.

I have a personal goal for myself that I follow; I only accept a leadership position when someone has asked me to be the leader. Not by my own agenda, but by the wishes of members in the group, company, family, or community I am being asked to serve.

Three Guiding Lessons

"One swing set, well worn but structurally sound, seeks new home. Make memories with your kid or kids so that someday he or she or they will look into the backyard and feel the ache of sentimentality as desperately as I did this afternoon. It's all fragile and fleeting, dear reader, but with this swing set, your child(ren) will be introduced to the ups and downs of human life gently and safely, and may also learn the most important lesson of all: No matter how hard you kick, no matter how high you get, you can't go all

the way around."

~ John Green, *The Fault in Our Stars*

My definition of success can really be found in three lessons that have shaped my life:

1. First, my guiding principle is something my father said years ago. He told me *"Don't do anything that will bring shame on the family."* A simple statement, but it guides me in most of my decisions. By following that rule it acts as a compass and barometer to test my actions against my ethics and morality.

2. The second is a goal I have for myself. I once heard that we should live our lives in the manner in which we would like to have our epithets to read on our gravestones. This is true, but I'd like to see some of the benefit of my work. In that vein, I have a vision myself as an old man in my 80's or 90's with a walker at some public ceremony where someone is being honored and the honoree upon receiving his or her award points to me in the crowd and says *"I was able to do this because something Marcus Mitchell said to me years ago, and it inspired me*

to take this path." That is one of my true goals that drive me to help others.

3. Lastly, I hold onto my own vision and personal definition of success. It's in the shape of a poem which is popularly attributed to Ralph Waldo Emerson; however I believe the true author is unknown. I keep a copy of it on my desk to remind me every day of my goals. It reads as follows:

"To laugh often and much
to win the respect of intelligent people
and affection of children; to earn the
appreciation of honest critics and
endure the betrayal of false friends;
to appreciate beauty, to find the best
in others; to leave the world a bit
better, whether by a healthy child
a garden patch or redeemed
social condition; to know even
one life has breathed easier because
you have lived. This is to have
succeeded."

I've learned over the years that a great leader must work to cultivate the relationships of the people around him or her. Networking is the key to building relationships with substance amongst the people you meet and work with. It is essential to leading.

It is a social aspect of being a Renaissance person, not just intellectual and professional accomplishments, but truly knowing people around you and loving them for the people they are, and not for the people you want them to be. Simple courtesies and mutual respect go a long way with building long-lasting friendships and relationships.

One must enter a leadership position with correct motivations, integrity, compassion and a genuine love for the people one is seeking to lead. One must use one's powers for good, not evil. The principle rule one must follow is: *Care for those you lead.*

Strength in People

"Leaders must be close enough to relate to others, but far enough ahead to motivate them."

~John C. Maxwell

The greatest strength a leader has is the will of his people to follow and execute steps and tasks towards a common goal. Inspiring people to do so requires that a leader constantly remind the group of the following:

- *Get them to know and look at the goal on the future horizon*
- *Have them envision the outcome*
- *Remind them constantly of the progress so as to motivate them further*
- *Celebrate the success and milestones as they are achieved*

These are the essential steps that a leader must remember to do on a regular basis to build the strength of his or her following. It is caring enough to remind them of the direction they are heading, how far they have come and how much closer they are to completion.

You will also see that strength comes in taking some time now and again to celebrate progress. Some goals can take months, or even years to obtain. Breaking down the goals into sub-goals or 'milestones' allows for progress to become visible to one and all, and also affords an opportunity to celebrate forward progress so that they can move onto the next milestone with vigor.

Chapter Fifteen:
Lessons Right in the Heart

In this final chapter, I have chosen to share the thoughts of inspiration from other people whose words of wisdom have so enriched my life as a leader.

Among the following lessons, some I will add commentary giving my insight and experience on how I applied those lessons in my life and the last section will stand alone as self evident statements of truth unto themselves.

Some of these lessons touch on the compassion of leadership, and others touch on the courage, motivation and strength a leader must have to be successful. I hope you will find as much inspiration as I have over the years with these profound words of wisdom.

ॐ

"I must follow the people. Am I not their leader?"

~Benjamin Disraeli

Benjamin Disraeli was a famous British Prime Minister who led his country through difficult times and social reform emphasizing mutual obligations toward members individually and across socio-economic lines. This quote is very interesting as it gives us a glimpse into his ideas and beliefs on leadership.

He views himself as a servant, subject to the will of his followers, and the instrument to secure their well-being. He will do what they want first above all things as a group, and be reluctant to impose his own agenda on the population at large.

"Leadership is the capacity to translate vision into reality."

~Warren Bennis

Very often it is a challenge to transition from the idea or concept to it evolving into a vision, and then ultimately to a realization of that vision. The leadership of any effort is responsible for creating a vision for the group to follow. The success of realizing the vision is the ability of leadership to define a critical path of action to reach that goal defined in the vision.

That, however, is the key. A critical path is the epitome of reality and practicalities for project management. Leaders must identify the critical path to success and consider the pitfalls, distractions, the resources available and needed personnel to accomplish the task. There must also be a timeline for any project or effort.

Obviously, these requirements require an honest and critical examination of all the facts available related to the task at hand. The leader must balance creativity and pragmatism to walk that critical path to success.

"A leader is a dealer in hope."

~Napoleon Bonaparte

Hope is the shining light, a beacon that a group can see from afar. Hope is an icon for people to focus on in their strides forward in life and in their endeavors.

A leader will facilitate hope and the challenges he or she and their people are presented. One must be able to articulate a method to realize the vision, and connect with the improved situation by accomplishing that vision which is represented through a sense of hope.

"Become the kind of leader that people would follow voluntarily; even if you had no title or position."

~Brian Tracy

This book is designed for people to take leadership advice and is composed of insights to enable the reader to be a leader from any position. I have mentioned at a few points throughout this book that leadership percolates to the top.

By exhibiting the qualities of leadership, a person will be able to lead a group of total strangers. Having an official title, or even your name, are not necessary to earn the respect of a group and be elevated to a position of leadership among them.

"To command is to serve, nothing more and nothing less."

~Andre Malraux

All great leaders are simply servants of their people. A leader must have love for others in order to sustain his ability and internal desire to serve his or her people.

The other motivation to lead may diminish over time, and with it, a diminishing of leadership and a willingness to follow.

"A good general not only sees the way to victory; he also knows when victory is impossible."

~Polybius

When leading a group of people toward any goal, there are bound to be challenges and risks. Otherwise, leadership would not be necessary. This condition is essential for a leader to exist.

We've already discussed the necessity for the leader to define and identify the critical path to success. The great leader must also recognize a path to destruction and failure, and take steps to correct a disastrous course.

Pyrrhus was a Greek General who was one of the strongest opponents of early Rome. He defeated the Romans at Heraclea in 280A.D. and Asculum in 279AD, but suffered his own ruinous losses.

Plutarch, a writer at the time, declared to Pyrrhus after the costly victory over the Romans, that another similar victory would destroy him.

Plutarch later coined a passage which has passed through the centuries in a collected biography he wrote on the lives of famous men which included Pyrrhus. The catchphrase was: *A Pyrrhic victory.* This refers to a goal or victory that is achieved at far too great a cost.

A great leader must recognize the sustainable success for his or her followers. Do not get caught up in battles or endeavors that come at too great a cost, as they do not offer successful sustainability and security for your followers.

"Leaders think and talk about the solutions. Followers think and talk about the problems."

~Brian Tracy

I have always found great value in group discussions along with brainstorming sessions when considering a challenge or problem. As I have mentioned before, I seek to hear the one comment that offers a solution instead of 10 comments describing the challenge.

An examination of the problem at hand is necessary, but that is not the reason for a council. One must adopt and cultivate a culture of critical thinking, problem solving and creating solutions. This leads to faster results and the marshaling of your resources to overcome any obstacles and help you reach your goals.

"A true leader has the confidence to stand alone, the courage to make tough decisions, and the compassion to listen to the needs of others. He does not set out to be a leader, but becomes one by the equality of his actions and the integrity of his intent."

~ Douglas MacArthur

This point speaks directly to the heart of my personal experience and leadership. Through the years I have considered myself a student, and sometimes I would take a point, or position, and stand against the majority of people around who were in opposition.

Indeed, many times I have stood alone.

The confidence to stand alone is not born of arrogance or pride, or need to prove that you are right. Confidence is born in the knowledge of one's self.

A leader must know all about himself. He must know one's own limitations, one's own strengths, needs and one's own self-imposed lines that they will not cross lines drawn in the sands of their own soul. He or she must know the purity of their own motivations.

With this confidence born of integrity, a true leader can make tough decisions, even unpopular decisions in the belief that he or she is making the best choices for the welfare of his followers.

They must study their followers by listening to what they say; their complaints, the criticism, the praise, their silence - what they do not say. They must also watch their actions and inactions.

Leadership is not a goal, but rather one is elevated to leadership through the true love one has and respect for the people around him.

"All of the great leaders have had one characteristic in common: it was the willingness to

confront unequivocally the major anxiety of their people in their time. This, and not much else, is the essence of leadership."

~John Kenneth Galbraith

The study of economics is also known as the dismal science. It examines the quest of human beings for resources and the dynamics that evolve from that quest.

As any group seeks resources; food, water, shelter, gasoline, land, increased revenues, prestige, etc. anxiety can be created. In those situations and circumstances leaders emerge to address those needs for the people they represent. This quote speaks to the essence of why leaders emerge.

"Great leaders are almost always great simplifiers, who can cut through argument, debate, and doubt to offer a solution everybody can understand."

~General Colin Powell

This message is so true. I frequently witnessed a leader emerge in the midst of a discussion or debate by offering concise and direct solutions without a lot of what could best be described as *editorial meanderings*. The comments are often very simple, leaving the other debaters questioning themselves and asking, *"Why did I not see that before?"* A great leader offers an epiphany.

"I cannot give you the formula for success, but I can give you the formula for failure, which is: Try to please everybody."

~Herbert Swope

Sometimes leaders make the mistake of trying to please everybody, driven by the love and compassion they have for their followers. It can also come from the misguided efforts of trying to be all things to all people in an effort to become popular.

This is a recipe for disaster. Operating this way will soon become an unsustainable leadership strategy as the leader using this will quickly lose the confidence of his followers.

"Leadership does not always wear the harness of compromise."

~Woodrow Wilson

I included this to further illustrate and explain the quote from Herbert Swope regarding pleasing everyone. A leader is not a dictator but may often be mistaken for one.

The leader has been selected by his followers to make tough decisions and provide clarity.

Sometimes a lack of resources and special circumstances in general necessitate a final decision for them to move forward on an issue. This is the leader's job and responsibility. It falls on him or her to make the final call.

"Leadership is solving problems. The day soldiers stop bringing you their problems is the day you have stopped leading them. They have either lost confidence that you can help or concluded you do not care. Either case is a failure of leadership."

~Colin Powell

This quote speaks for itself. A leader should always be approachable, and never aloof. The leader should not lament his followers presenting problems to him for his attention.

He or she should praise them and thank them for having confidence that he may be able to provide solutions. A leader should thank them for their respect and willingness to reach out to them for advice.

"You gain strength, courage and confidence by every experience in which you really stop to look fear in the face. You must do the thing you think you cannot do."

~Eleanor Roosevelt

Strength, courage and confidence are gained sometimes through hardship. Leaders and followers alike are vetted through tough times and challenges.

There's an expression that I like to remember: *"Tough times don't last, tough people do"*. A leader is often defined by the hardship that he faces and grapples with head on, unabashedly.

Inspiring Quotes that Stand Alone

"A leader takes people where they want to go. A great leader takes people where they don't necessarily want to go, but ought to be."

~Rosalynn Carter

"A leader is one who knows the way, goes the way, and shows the way."

~John Maxwell

"My own definition of leadership is this: The capacity and the will to rally men and women to a common purpose and the character which inspires confidence."
~General Montgomery

"A true leader has the confidence to stand alone, the courage to make tough decisions, and the compassion to listen to the needs of others. He does not set out to be a leader, but becomes one by the equality of his actions and the integrity of his intent."
~Douglas MacArthur

"Where there is no vision, the people perish."

~Proverbs 29:18

"We live in a society obsessed with public opinion. But leadership has never been about popularity."
~Marco Rubio

"There are three essentials to leadership: humility, clarity and courage."

~Fuchan Yuan

"My responsibility is getting all my players playing for the name on the front of the jersey, not the one on the back."

~Author Unknown

❧Summary❧

This book has been a culmination of many years of personal experience, observation, hardship and hard knocks. I have enjoyed every step of the way, the ups and downs, peaks and valleys, joys and hardships. My hope is that this book has offered you as a reader insightful advice as well as a hand through times of adversity.

Leadership as you have learned has many facets: *Courage, determination, motivation, compassion, wisdom, intelligence, adversity, responsibility, vision* and *planning* to name but a few. It does not require a special internal gift that one must be born with to become a leader, it just takes willingness to rise to the occasion and be in control.

As you have witnessed throughout the pages of this book, I have cited and quoted many sources from many great references and people both contemporary and from history. A leader cannot become a great leader alone. The stage is never bare. One must rely on the wisdom of our forbearers.

To be successful as a leader, one must be willing to stand on the shoulders of geniuses, and embrace the hand of guidance offering knowledge and wisdom. To shut oneself off from the fruits of the experiences and insights of others is to embark on the path to failure and obscurity.

Leadership therefore is a continual learning experience. It is a vibrant activity, and a constant interaction with life. Always seek to better ones own understanding, and keep the door open for constant learning, and you will be on the path to greatness.

In the introduction of this book, I mentioned one of my many mottos that I have used in countless groups I have led. I will close this book by repeating it here, and it is simply this:

"Make It Happen!"

About the Author

Marcus Mitchell, a resident of Providence Rhode Island's East Side, is an active board member on various organizations including serving as the Founding President of the Providence Community Library, as a Board member on the Miriam Hospital Board of Governors and other community and nationally based organizations continuing his love for community service.

Often sought by government and corporate leaders for his years of experience, he wields a wealth of community development and policy expertise, along with decades of experience in Corporate Strategy. Mitchell has also co-authored 16 scientific publications over 15yrs of cardiovascular scientific research and is the founding President of the National Urban League Young Professionals, with dozens of chapters and thousands of members across the country.

In the United States Coast Guard Auxiliary, he served as a flotilla commander; today he still actively promotes and supports environmental education programs and protection strategies, search and rescue patrols and disaster readiness.

He enjoys leveraging his economic development, business creations, leadership and coalition building skills in national and international arenas, specifically within government, corporate, philanthropic and political strategy efforts to enhance communities around the country.

He is the Founder of *Shere Strategy Enterprises*, a strategic solutions company, with focus areas in crisis management, small business start-ups and conflict resolution. In his free time with his family, he enjoys sailing, flying, camping and good conversation.

Shere Strategy Enterprises
Marcus Mitchell - Principal Executive
www.Shere-Enterprises.com
mpm@shere-enterprises.com

CPSIA information can be obtained at www.ICGtesting.com
Printed in the USA
LVOW12s1736080414

380833LV00006B/860/P

9 781495 990595